blue
rider
press

the
asylum

also by simon doonan

Gay Men Don't Get Fat
Eccentric Glamour
Wacky Chicks
Beautiful People (originally published as *Nasty*)
Confessions of a Window Dresser

the
asylum

a collage of couture
reminiscences . . . and hysteria

SIMON DOONAN

BLUE RIDER PRESS
A MEMBER OF PENGUIN GROUP (USA)
NEW YORK

blue
rider
press

Published by the Penguin Group

Penguin Group (USA), 375 Hudson Street,
New York, New York 10014, USA

USA · Canada · UK · Ireland · Australia
New Zealand · India · South Africa · China

Penguin Books Ltd, Registered Offices: 80 Strand, London WC2R 0RL, England
For more information about the Penguin Group visit penguin.com

Library of Congress Cataloging-in-Publication Data

Doonan, Simon, date.
The asylum : a collage of couture reminiscences / Simon Doonan.
p.   cm
ISBN 978-0-399-16189-6 (hardback)
1. Clothing and dress—Humor.   2. Fashion—Humor.   I. Title.
TT507.D585   2013   2013015426
746.9'20207—dc23

Printed in the United States of America
1   3   5   7   9   10   8   6   4   2

Book design by Stephanie Huntwork

Penguin is committed to publishing works of quality and integrity. In that spirit,
we are proud to offer this book to our readers; however, the story,
the experiences, and the words are the author's alone.

FOR JONNY

contents

author's note

AH! FASHION.

A nuthouse? A refuge? Or maybe both. Yes, an asylum in both senses of the word. A place where unemployable crazy people are always welcome.

Every seasoned fashion personage has his or her favorite stories of folly, aberration, derangement, kookiness and excess.

These are mine.

In most instances real names are used. I have tweaked the identities of certain individuals to protect their innocence and cherish their fabulosity.

Have I embroidered or embellished? Let me answer that question by quoting Diana Vreeland: "Exaggeration is my only reality."

—S. D.

Get on to Princess Anne's people and tell her that everybody there will be mentally ill. Tell her we'll sponsor her to wear a designer dress, okay? And make sure she realizes that if she doesn't wear it those little children won't get anything.

—Edina, planning a fashion event on the
first episode of *Absolutely Fabulous*

the
asylum

lipstick on your kneecaps

CATHERINE DENEUVE is walking around West London with a skinned rabbit in her purse. A decaying skinned rabbit. She is in a zombified state, twitching and hallucinating. In Polanski's legendarily bizarre movie *Repulsion*, Mademoiselle Deneuve has clearly lost her mind, and yet . . . has she ever looked chicer? With her pale understated clothing, her luscious blond tresses and her fabulously blank facial expression, she is the epitome of sixties French preppy cool.

Fashion and madness. Strange bedfellows. Or are they?

I have a close friend who works in a nuthouse, let's call her Lizzie. While I skip about at fashion shoots and whoosh into the front row of runway shows, my hardworking psychologist pal toils in a seriously grim public mental asylum.

Over the years, Lizzie and I have kibitzed endlessly about work. The yawning chasm between our respective professional milieus has always provided us with much conversational fodder.

Logic dictates that these two glaringly contrasting worlds would have about as much in common as Big Ang and Mrs. Petraeus. What could be farther apart than the pampered artifice of fashion and the gritty melancholy of daily life in a public psychiatric facility?

And yet . . .

Time and again we find eerie similarities between these two worlds. Comparing and contrasting the goings-on in the world of fashion with the shenanigans of the folks at Lizzie's house of horrors proves both surreal and illuminating.

Having come from a long line of lunatics—my genes are liberally accessorized with manic depression and schizophrenia—I have a special interest in madness. The fear that I might follow the family tradition and start carrying a skinned rodent in my purse, even metaphorically, began in childhood and has dogged me my entire life. Perhaps one day I will wake up and be overcome with *Weltschmerz* like Grandpa Doonan or drunken Uncle Dave and simply off myself. Or maybe I will lose my noodle like Uncle Ken and end up strapped to a board, receiving electric-shock treatment. Or a lobotomy, just like Granny. These nagging dreads have produced in me an abiding interest in psychiatric disorders, which itself borders on psychiatric disorder.

Lizzie has always reciprocated my interest in her asylum with an equal curiosity about my world, the realm of style. Like many a single gal living in Manhattan, Lizzie regularly succumbs to the transformative charms of La Mode. I fuel her growing passion by giving her my old fashion magazines, which she enthusiastically devours over lunch in the mental hospital's cafeteria. As often as not, she has questions about what she reads.

First and foremost, Lizzie is repeatedly struck by the concept of "trends." Perturbed, you might almost say. She tears out pages and waves them at me in a nutty, hostile manner.

"It says here that, quote, 'Everyone is wearing fishnets . . . again.'"

"It's a big trend for spring."

"No, it isn't. You are hallucinating. I haven't seen anyone in Manhattan wearing fishnets, except the old tranny hooker on my block. How long have you fashion people been harboring this particular delusion?"

"Calm down."

"You need to realize that my hospital is full of people who imagine crazy shit. They see patterns where there are none."

Seeing patterns where there are none. In Lizzie's profession, insisting upon the existence of patterns of any kind constitutes a diagnostic red flag, a symptom of a fairly serious psychiatric disorder. But not for me. I have long since habituated to the idea of trends and have always taken great pleasure in catapulting them at Lizzie.

Fluorescent colors are happening *right now*. I'm seeing them everywhere.

Black rubber trench coats? Who isn't wearing one?

Angora is BACK! Everyone knows that.

Snakeskin hobos! Don't mind if I do.

For me, these trends are little more than innocuous ejaculations. To Lizzie, they seem quite sinister. If somebody starts seeing trends—seeing patterns where none are objectively verifiable—then that particular somebody might need to be "sectioned."

"You're seeing fluorescents everywhere? Lots of our new arrivals say stuff like that. Usually they're schizophrenic. But sometimes they've just come off a glue-huffing binge. It takes a while to figure it out."

Grudgingly, I am willing to admit to Lizzie that we fashion people can be a tad dogmatic. Yes, the trends that shriek at the reader from the pages of today's magazines are somewhat overstated and repetitive. Military coats! Futuristic footwear! Couture pouf skirts! Boho caftans! Again! How, I often ask myself, can leopard print constitute "an important new trend" when it's been "an important new trend" for the last ten years?

One can just see the harried fashion editors, aided by legions of assistants, laying out the forty million runway images from any given season and, based on an arbitrary and statistically insignificant sampling, starting to "see patterns."

"Look, here's an orange skirt at Céline. And look, an orange purse at Prada. Hold the presses! I'm seeing a pattern here . . ."

"Yes, but we told our readers that orange was *the* trend last season . . ."

"Zip it!"

When the trends of the season are unfurled online or in magazines, they can seem forced or a tad bogus. But are they an indication that somebody needs to be strapped to a board and given electric-shock treatment? Not really. What seems like madness to Lizzie—seeing patterns where there are none—is really just a sincere attempt to impose a soupçon of structure. The fashion landscape is, after all, a wacky and ever-expanding place which can seem daunting and quite bloblike, as in *The Blob*, the idiotic fifties sci-fi movie about a giant growing amoeba which tries to eat Steve McQueen and engulf the world. Those trend reports are nothing more than a gung-ho effort to provide the hordes of jolly fashion consumers with a few helpful guidelines. Is that so wrong?

Some mental health professionals will tell you that the exact same process is going on in the mind of a psychiatric patient. The imposing of patterns and rules, no matter how strange or illogical, provides a buffer against all the blobby chaos. Take that, Doctor Lizzie! I can play shrink too!

As you can probably tell by now, Lizzie and I are locked in an irrational-but-enjoyable big dick contest. Whose world is more demented? The world of the insane or the world of the insanely fashionable? On some occasions we are out to prove that our own world is saner. More often than not we are hell-bent on one-upping and out-crazying each other.

The denizens of both our worlds often suffer from a bad case of *folie de grandeur*. Whenever I regale Lizzie with an instance of preposterous fashion grandiosity, she is always able to top it. I once complained to her about some asshole designer who constantly referred to himself in the third person and brayed on about his global brand domination. Lizzie responded: "You think your fashion freaks are getting too big for their bustiers. Pah! That's nothing. Today I chatted with a patient who told me he was totally exhausted. When I asked him why, he said that he was tired of running both the FBI and the CIA."

Not only are Lizzie's patients grandiose, they can be quite snarky. I am frequently taken aback by their inclination to play fashion police and express disdain at the appearances and style choices of others. They are, as it turns out, just as prone to making cutting remarks as any blogger or Fashion Week attendee, if not more so.

Entering a group therapy session, Lizzie is invariably greeted with a series of subtly lacerating comments about her personal appearance.

"Dr. Lizzie, your skin is looking better today."

"But you are getting a bit thick, Doctor."

"Don't listen to him, Doc. Yes, you're looking a little thick, but I like my bitches that way."

Individual therapy sessions bring forth an even more fearsome candor. Something about the intimacy of these settings seems to give Lizzie's patients carte blanche to be downright evil.

One particular lady stands out. Let's call her Patient X. Homeless and OxyContin-addicted, Patient X arrived at the hospital in a state of abject physical and mental disintegration. Within days, thanks to medication, food, and shelter, she made startling improvements in all areas, especially her critical faculties. And by critical, I do mean *critical*.

"It's great to see you looking so well."

"Thanks, Doc. Right back atcha! By the way, nice boots!"

Lizzie had recently splurged on a pair of platform boots after being advised by yours truly that they were a current trend. The compliment served to alleviate some of her misgivings about whether the boot trend might have been real or imagined.

"Thanks. I'm glad you like them."

"You know what, Doc," said X, leaning back in her chair and snapping her gum. "When I get out of this dump, I'm going to buy myself a pair of moderately priced boots . . . just like yours."

When Lizzie later regaled me with this story, I was less than sympathetic, assuring her in no uncertain terms that this kind of double-edged noncompliment is very common in my world.

"I love your Pucci leggings. But for the office? Maybe better for the weekend. Or Halloween. *Non?*"

Back to boots.

Boots have, for some reason, caused Lizzie to be the brunt of endless gibes. In the course of assessing one particular patient's ability to think abstractly, she asked him, "Do you know the expression 'You can't judge a book by its cover'? What do you think it means?"

Slowly and thoughtfully, he looked Lizzie up and down. Then his eyes alighted on her boots, which, as chance would have it, were extremely beaten-up.

Without moving his gaze, he said, "It means you can't judge someone by how they look on the outside . . . but sometimes you can, if you know what I mean."

His gaze remained fixed on those scuffed boots.

"That's all I will say for now. I've got to go."

Next time Lizzie saw this particular patient, she purposely wore boots that were unscuffed. They were, in fact, the "moderately priced boots" referred to earlier.

The patient eyed the fresh new footwear and spoke. "Doc, I think you're starting to put your best foot forward, if you know what I mean."

When summer rolled around, and boot season was just a distant memory, Lizzie anticipated a break in the critical onslaught. 'Twas not to be.

"Hey, Doc, I like your sandals."

"Thank you."

"Where did you get them?"

"I forget. Somewhere Downtown."

"Thom McAn! For five dollars!"

The patient then walked away laughing to himself.

Eccentricity and extremism are common in Lizzie's world. They are also the foundation of great style. The bold avatars of fashion—the Daphne Guinnesses, the Michelle Harpers and the Tilda Swintons—propel the evolution of fashion forward by daring to enrobe themselves in a way which may well look clowny and loopy to the Katie Courics of the world. Then, five years later, the Katie Courics are wearing some version of that original wackadoodly ensemble.

Unlike regular folk, mental patients have a strong, albeit unwitting, tolerance and affinity for avant-garde style. Schizophrenics often concoct headwraps that are reminiscent of Comme des Garçons, Lady Gaga or Erykah Badu. Bipolar folk love yellow eye shadow just as much as Nicki Minaj does. The hallways of Lizzie's hospital are a veritable runway show of experimental flamboyance.

Lizzie's young interns were so blown away by the unconscious fashion daring of the arriving patients that they were inspired to invent a game called "Inpatient or Williamsburg Hipster?" The typical patient might have a beard down to his waist, a shrunken flannel shirt and ill-fitting suit pants. *Et voilà!* "Inpatient or Williamsburg Hipster?"

Lizzie is best able to observe the avant-gardism and stylish verve of her patients on "grooming day." When I first heard that one day a week is set aside for a little on-premises vanity and primping, I was anxious to help. I believe in the curative powers of what my mother used to call "getting a bit tarted up." When people get depressed, the first thing to go is their vanity. There's no question that a little lippy, or a fake lash or two, can act as a mood elevator.

I mentioned Lizzie's grooming day to my friend François Nars. He too became enthused and committed to helping Lizzie's patients. The next day a luxurious assortment of Nars maquillage arrived on my doorstep. I forwarded it immediately to Lizzie so that she would have it in time for grooming day. When I saw her a week later, I was anxious to find out how it all went.

"The patients loved the Nars makeup."

"Do you have pics I can forward to François?"

"I don't think he would be too happy. Most of the lipstick ended up on their foreheads and the backs of their legs."

"François is a creative fashion dude. He would probably find it inspiring."

"You people are sick."

There's that undercurrent of competitive hostility again. Whose world is the more freaky? The nuthouse or the runway?

Once, I called Lizzie from a photo shoot to say hey. I told her that we were photographing some of Barneys' fall merchandise for a direct-mail catalog and that we were taking our inspiration from *Grey Gardens*. When she told me she hadn't seen it, I launched into an enthusiastic gush about this legendary seventies Maysles brothers documentary about a mother and daughter who lived in Havisham-esque decay in East Hampton.

"It's so major. You won't believe the styling. These two broads—cousins of Jackie Onassis!—are called Little Edie and

Big Edie, and they should have been editing a groovy alternative fashion magazine or designing clothes. They are the ultimate stylists."

The following weekend Lizzie rented the movie. I waited for her feedback with white knuckles. My phone jangled late on Sunday night.

"Wasn't it fabulous! Didn't you love it to bits?"

"Fabulous? You sick fuck! I see women like Little Edie wearing sweaters wrapped around their heads all day long. It usually indicates that they're at the end of their rope and are trying to muffle the voices in their heads. When I watched this movie, all I saw were potential symptoms of schizophrenia and suffering, and all you can see are styling tips. You fashion people are just as twisted as any of my patients."

I accepted Lizzie's admonishment. There was no denying the accuracy of her brutal assessment of La Mode and me. However, along with feeling appropriately castigated, I also felt a tingle of triumph and solidarity. I was happy to be diagnosed at the wrong end of the sanity spectrum, waving and smiling, and proudly carrying a skinned rabbit in my man-bag.

from couture
to parole

FASHION DESIGNERS enjoy dating hustlers and porn stars. There's no need to name names. Take a gander at "Page Six" and you will find no shortage of sizzling designer dalliances.

This situation is nothing new. These shady couplings are as integral to the world of style as raw seams and bulimia. We fashion people have an insatiable and irrational craving for both high and low experiences. The luxe versus the louche. The classy and the déclassé. The *nostalgie de la boue*. We take our inspiration from both the blighted and the baroque.

Before Mayor Giuliani did his big nineties cleanup, before the glamification of the meat market and before the Disneyfication of Times Square, there was no shortage of sordid nocturnal hangouts in New York City. These charming crap holes were mostly leftovers from the hedonistic seventies and were frequented by feral perverts, drug-addled hustlers, crazed crossdressers and me . . . and people like me. Who were we? We were style addicts in search of glamour.

If you wanted to run into all your fashion pals and colleagues and do a spot of networking, then all you had to do was follow the unsavory folk, the if-Diane-Arbus-were-still-alive-she-would-be-photographing-me people. I am talking about the outsider freaks and ne'er-do-wells who have always made New York such a rich source of stylish inspiration.

There was Edelweiss, a club for violence-prone tranny hookers and the men who adored them. In a similar vein, there was Sally's Hideaway, located incongruously right opposite the back entrance of the old *New York Times* building. There was L'Escualita, a scorching Latin cabaret disco where arriving patrons were checked for knives before they passed through a turnstile.

I associate L'Escualita with a certain dermatological catastrophe. One time I was leaning against a column enjoying the drag show. The performer exhorted us all to sit on the floor so that those at the back would have a better view. I slid obediently downward. A protruding rusty nail gouged a mole off my back. It hurt.

Half a mile east of L'Escualita was a male strip club, tucked behind the Howard Johnson's coffee shop—fried clams anyone?—on Times Square. It was called the Gaiety.

The Gaiety was chic, petite, very bijou and somewhat roach-infested. The cost of entry was ten dollars, paid through a gruesome little pawn-broker grille. Mimicking Candy Darling in Andy Warhol's movie *Flesh*, we habitués would Frenchify the cost with an indignant "Ten dolluuuurs?"

Inside was a decaying burlesque theater with about twenty rows of seats and a small stage. To the left of the auditorium was a narrow archway which opened up upon a cozy mingling zone known as the "Fantasy Lounge."

I am proud to say that I was a regular. I spent many evenings gossiping in the red velvet seats and watching the old geezers in the front row getting tea-bagged by the more enthusiastic interactive performers.

For many fashion people, this sordid but undeniably charming boîte was a social club, a place to chill after a week of stress and pinking shears. It was a place where everybody knew your name. Speaking of names: Marc Jacobs, Thierry Mugler, Susanne Bartsch, Calvin Klein, Kerry Warn, Joey Arias, Freddie Leiba, Rifat Ozbek, Henny Garfunkel, Larissa, Luciana Martinez, Edwige, Steven Meisel, Madonna—the names of the illustrious fashionrati who popped into the Gaiety to mingle with *les misérables* and enjoy the strip show was a long and impressive one. Madge loved it so much she elected to use it as a location for her 1992 *Sex* book.

The burlesques at the Gaiety were mysteriously overseen by an invisible host who announced the various performers via a fuzzy, malfunctioning public address system. His signature flourish was to always repeat the name of the upcoming stripper—his mouth was always much too close to the microphone—with tremendous and often unwarranted theatrical gravitas.

"And *now*, directly from a sold-out run at the Manhole in Detroit, we bring you . . . Anton . . . *Anton . . . ANTON!*"

The young man in question, whose name was probably Kevin, would saunter on stage and begin to flaunt himself, disrobing in time to the music. By today's Internet porn standards, the performances were quite tame. The only outré moment occurred at the end of the show when all the lads came on stage for the hard-on finale.

After the show, the invisible host encouraged us audience members to decamp to the Fantasy Lounge for refreshments and the opportunity to meet and mingle with the various "performers."

The complimentary snacks consisted of a bowl of fruit punch, served in a banquet-size cut-plastic bowl with cups dangling around the perimeter, and a mound of pretzels dumped unceremoniously onto an oversize vacuum-formed silver plastic charger. I never partook of these offerings. You never knew where they'd been. Ditto the dancing boys and hustlers.

One night I got chatted up by a nice lad, a West Point cadet, who was straight but "needed extra cash for the wife and kids." He zipped up to New York every weekend for a little relaxation at the Gaiety.

Every lad at the Gaiety had an equally preposterous backstory: "I'm not really sleeping in the Port Authority Bus Terminal and living out of vending machines. Oh no. I'm a goal-oriented West Point cadet with a wholesome wife and kids waiting at home."

With visions of moi being strangled and thrown in the East River, I declined his offer of "a night of fun."

Not everyone shared my sense of caution. My roommate Henry, for example.

Henry and I were not lovers. (Perish the thought!) He was more like a big sister, a big, generous, recklessly fabulous, you-won't-believe-what-she-did-now sister.

Henry was—and remains to this day—a much-in-demand

fashion publicist. Older and more established than I was, he always impressed me with his breezy confidence and his international savoir faire. He is Eddie *and* Patsy *and* Bubble combined.

The Gaiety boys were always responsive to Henry's brand of sassy badinage. His cheeky, blunt manner brought out the best in even the most sociopathic stripper. When they clustered around him, I felt like I was watching Mae West being inundated by horny sailors on leave.

It was inevitable that Henry would fall for one of these grifting Adonises. And fall he did.

Cue the lights. Enter Danny.

Some hustlers are so rough and butch it is hard to tell that they are gay. Danny was one such person. Gay is the last word which sprang to mind. Danny was a circus act of chest-beating masculine gender performance. When, years later, *The Wire* became the addiction du jour, those corner boys reminded me of Danny. He embodied the scariest bits of Spanish Harlem, the Bronx and Bed-Stuy. He was terrifying. But not to Henry.

From the moment Henry strolled into the Fantasy Lounge and met Danny—their eyes locking across a bowl of fetid punch and a mound of stale pretzels—they became a unit.

Sometimes when a foncy person (Henry) meets a street person (Danny), the foncy person keeps the street person at an arm's length. With a commendable egalitarian spirit, Henry enthusiastically integrated Danny into his life—and mine.

Danny hung out at our apartment. Danny ate brekkie. Danny yelled at the telly. Danny threw things out of the window. Danny came to chichi cocktail parties hosted by Henry's fashion friends. Danny even came on vacation with us.

Miami was our usual destination. As soon as we arrived, Danny would jump into the rental car, sans driver's license, and roar over the causeway. With James Brown's "Party Time" blasting, he would speed up dramatically and then slow down and make the car dance in time to the music by thumping the accelerator.

It's pahty tahme! Thump! Thump! Thump!

It's pahty tahme! Thump! Thump! Thump!

I have vivid memories of jiggling up and down and lurching backward and forward, with a pregnant Susanne Bartsch in the backseat, begging for mercy in the name of her unborn child. I sat in the front seat, preparing to barf into my vintage resort tote and whimpering audibly. And Henry? He was screaming with laughter. He was having a ball.

We always stayed at the Raleigh in South Beach. Today it's a super-glam, dreamy, Kardashian-ish joint. Back then it was undergoing a slow, yeasty, moldy renovation. However, the crappy carpets and the disintegrating plumbing were more than made up for by the incredible pool. The deco-aquatic Busby Berkeley fantasia provided the backdrop for many of the eighties and early nineties Versace print advertising campaigns. The fashion crowd loved it, as did Mickey Rourke, who was often to be found lounging poolside with his beloved Chihuahuas on gold and leopard-print leashes.

New Year's Day in the early nineties.

Danny insisted that we leave the poolside glamour and go fishing. This surprised me. I hadn't pegged him for the Ernest Hemingway type.

We pahty tahmed our way down to some harbor or other

where Henry, Danny, and I boarded a little rented cruiser and headed out to sea. This, I mused, would be a key moment in what was clearly turning into a *Dateline NBC* story. "The three friends went fishing under a cloudless sky. But only one of them made it back to the port. His name was D . . ."

But Danny was incapable of much activity on this particular morning. He was knackered. Having been out till the wee hours, he collapsed into a deep sleep. With his strapping god-like physique and his dusky complexion, the recumbent Danny looked like an exhausted Nubian from the orgy scene in *Fellini Satyricon*.

We reached our destination. Henry alerted the sleeping Danny to this fact by slapping him across the face with a smelly sardine from the bait box. I braced myself for a horrible maritime confrontation. The idea of provoking Danny with a decomposing fish seemed nothing short of suicidal.

Danny leapt to his feet and assumed a posture that suggested he might be about to get Ripley on Henry's ass. Henry stared right back at him, threw another fish and cackled with mirth. Danny paused, wiping fish slime off his face, and then he laughed too.

While Henry curled up with a *Vogue*, Danny and I grabbed our rods. He proved to be a proficient fisherman. Much of his energy went into mocking my ineptitude and my sluggishness.

"Faggot! Hurry the motherfuck up!" said Danny. "The other fuckers are going to eat your fucker."

Danny was correct. Each time I reeled in a fish, all that remained of my catch was a dangling head.

"Where did you learn to fish?" I asked.

"Some Fresh Air Fund bullshee-eeet."

By the time we chugged back into the harbor, Danny was in possession of a whole passel of mackerel and bluefish. His prize catch was a three-foot, hideously stinking sturgeon or grouper-type fish which bore more than a passing resemblance to Winston Churchill. Danny clutched it as if it were a newborn baby.

Later that day I was lounging by the pool, chatting with Carlyne Cerf de Dudzeele.

Carlyne is one of the legendary eccentrics of fashion. She is blonde, tanned, and wears an enormous number of gold bangles and, as if that were not enough, she single-handedly popularized the use of the phrase *"J'adore!"* The global usage of this phrase—there is even a perfume named J'adore!—can be traced back to the flamboyant Carlyne.

She has always brought great nuance to the use of this phrase. You can tell how much she adores something by how drawn out her delivery is. Under normal circumstances the *"j'a"* is usually followed by a slightly extended pause . . . then comes the *"DORE!"* But when Carlyne really, really, really adores something, an explosive *"J'AAA"* might be followed by a full minute of nail-biting suspense and then relief! Like a giant washing machine suddenly emptying, out pours the *"DORE!"* This signifies that the object of her affection is causing her to have a stroke.

Suddenly I heard a contretemps across the other side of the pool.

Carlyne and I looked over to see Danny.

"J'AAA. . . . .

. . . .

. . . .
. . . .
. . . .
. . . . *DORE!*" shrieked a greatly amused Carlyne, hurling both bracelet-encrusted arms heavenward, having let out her most extended *J'adore* ever.

Danny was on the opposite side of the pool, carrying his massive prehistoric-looking prize fish. He was walking from lounger to lounger. His goal? He wanted to turn Winston into some hard cash.

Sunbathers were being roused from their slumber, not with a spritz of Evian and the offer of a piña colada, but by Danny asking them to "check this mother out."

We watched in amazement as he reached Donatella Versace. Back then, before the construction of the famous Versace mansion, Donatella would sleep at the Fontainebleau (the closets were bigger) and lounge by the pool and oversee her shoots at the Raleigh. Danny tapped her on the shoulder and shoved Winnie in her face.

"Hey! Lady! Check this out. A hundred bucks."

Her visage was a picture of disdain. She waved him away with the hauteur of a great Italian principessa.

When Danny reached me, I politely declined and asked him what he had done with all the other fish.

"She wrapped them in my *Women's Wear Daily*s and stuffed them inside the minibar," yelled Henry, who loved to refer to Danny as "she" and who was watching the unfolding Benny Hill scene with great amusement from behind a gigantic rubber plant.

. . .

NOT ONLY WAS DANNY integrated into Henry's vacations and his tussy-flossy fashion milieu, but he also hung with the folks, by which I mean Henry's mother.

Henry's mother, Doris, was a regular visitor to our apartment in New York. She was a plain-speaking broad who hailed from the north of England. Doris had long since ceased to be shocked by her son and was more than familiar with his high-low lifestyle. She was quite accepting. Just don't touch her Rice-A-Roni.

The Rice-A-Roni debacle is indelibly etched in my mind. On this particular occasion Doris had just come from visiting relatives in San Francisco. She was on her way home to England and had stopped off in New York to check in with Henry and meet his new friend.

Doris was unsure of what to make of Danny. She was non-committal, and understandably so. Since Doris had a thick regional accent and Danny spoke in the patois of the streets, neither was able to understand the other, which was probably just as well.

Henry took Doris to the Hamptons for "a mother-daughter weekend" of high-thread-count sheets and Barefoot Contessa prepared foods. I headed to Fire Island, where I spent the weekend stuck, intermittently, to a black vinyl couch. (Clarification, dear reader, will be yours when you read the upcoming Suzy Menkes chapter.) Rashly, we left Danny alone in the apartment for an entire weekend.

We all returned to Manhattan on Sunday night from our

respective destinations with a certain level of apprehension. Would Danny have absconded with the contents of the apartment? Maybe he had trashed the place. Maybe he had gone fishing in the East River and stuffed the fridge with bloated bream.

Danny was nowhere to be seen. He was out having pahty tahme somewhere or other. However, we were relieved to note that the place looked perfectly tidy and normal. Good old Danny. How unfair it was to always assume the worst.

Mother Doris disappeared into Henry's bedroom and began repacking her suitcase for her UK flight the next day. After a few minutes, she let out a shriek of horror.

"He's stolen it! Two packets. I bought it in San Francisco specially!"

Doris ran into the kitchen, rummaged in the trash can and pulled out two empty Rice-A-Roni boxes. She held them aloft. The expression on her face was much more *"J'accuse!"* than *"J'adore!"*

"You can only get it in San Francisco. The man in the shop said. And he—*he*—bloody ate it!"

Doris finally calmed down when we took her to the D'Agostino across the street and showed her the shelves and shelves of Rice-A-Roni variants.

"Why the bloody hell do they call it 'the San Francisco treat.' It's bloody confusing. Stupid bloody Americans."

THE FOLLOWING SPRING we planned our usual trip to Miami. Danny seemed even more volatile than usual. Right before departing, he and Henry had a face-off. A bitchy comment sent Danny into a butch tizzy. He made a fist.

"Go on, hit me! It's what everyone said you would do eventually," said Henry, sounding very Susan Hayward and film noir—ish. Danny responded by punching a hole in the faux-finished terra-cotta wall behind Henry. (Don't judge our décor too harshly. Yes, it does sound very naff, but faux finishes were big back then, especially marbling and gold leafing.)

Down in Florida, Henry and Danny became night owls. We were on separate schedules. I lost track of them.

On the third day I started to crave a little drama. I wandered down the beach, thinking I might bump into the two lovebirds in our usual spot in front of the Raleigh.

Donatella was shooting with Bruce Weber on the beach. Lucie and Daniel de la Falaise were frolicking with white tigers while half-naked boys bounced up and down on trampolines in the background.

In the gaggle of spectators, I saw a mutual friend who filled me in.

"Danny's in jail in downtown Miami. He tried to knife a cop."

I felt a wave of relief. Danny's imprisonment was not exactly desirable, but maybe it would set Henry free from the bondage of this exhausting relationship. He was going to end up in the clink sooner or later. Pahty tahme could not go on forever.

Or could it?

Danny's incarceration did nothing to cool Henry's ardor. Au contraire! I think it actually heated things up. Henry found it HOT.

He spent the next few months commuting to Miami, visiting Danny and doing everything and anything—I am sure he toyed with baking a chocolate gâteau with a metal file inside—to get him out of jail.

After those first few months, Danny was transferred to a facility in upstate New York. Henry spent every weekend dutifully schlepping back and forth, taking a bus to a train to a ferry to a train to a bus, all for a half-hour nonconjugal visit.

Henry seemed to enjoy these seemingly masochistic trips. He told me that he loved to chat with the other broads—note I said "other"—on the bus. They shared feelings of solidarity and beleaguered wifely devotion, plus a few beauty tips.

"No, I haven't had time to get my roots done either. And our men all expect us to look our best. They don't realize what it takes to run a home and keep it together. Aren't you just *so* tired!"

Eventually Danny became eligible for parole. Henry attended the first hearing and voiced his unconditional support for his man.

"And what is *your* relationship to the defendant?" asked the presiding judge, while peering at Henry—he was sporting Maharishi embellished jeans, a charcoal-black Helmut Lang cotton jacket, Hermès espadrilles, a scarf made from Indian sari fabric, massive Cutler and Gross shades and an elephant-scrotum-size Fendi tote—with undisguised curiosity.

"She's my bitch!" interjected Danny. (Much tittering in the courtroom.)

Henry leapt at the chance to facilitate this process by becoming Danny's parole buddy, or whatever the hell it's called. In other words, Henry guaranteed the parole board he'd put a roof over Danny's head, and if Danny murdered anyone or destroyed any rental cars by making them dance to James Brown, then Henry would take full responsibility. All of Henry's friends joined in a Greek chorus imploring him not to be his guarantor. But Henry was adamant.

"Girls! You have to stand by your man."

The prison bureaucracy was cumbersome. Henry's gay nerves were severely tested. When a letter finally arrived bearing the date for Danny's parole hearing, Henry let out a massive sigh—and then a shriek of horror.

"Fuck! That's the same day as the couture show!"

At this point, Henry was working for a top fashion house. In addition to the twice-yearly prêt-à-porter collections, this particular *maison* also produced, with great verve and much pomp and circumstance, a legendary couture collection. Chichi socialites, movie celebs and wealthy Saudis made the pilgrimage to buy $40,000 frocks as if they were Twizzlers.

The date was set. The models were booked, as were the clients' suites at the Ritz. Even Helen Keller could see that there was no way to reschedule the couture show. There was only one thing for it: the parole date would have to be delayed.

Listening to Henry on the phone negotiating the date change with the prison officials, painstakingly explaining the importance of the couture show to fashion, and to the whole of humanity, was one of the most sublime moments of my life.

Naturally, he was successful. As a result of Henry's finagling, Danny became the only convicted felon in U.S. legal history whose parole date was dictated by the French couture calendar.

When the show was finished, Henry flew home and so did Danny, and the melodrama resumed once more.

When Danny dropped dead, it was not a huge surprise. Though he was a strapping hunk, he had a long history with drugs. One of his favorite tricks was to snort cocaine, yell "It's pahty tahme!" and then hit the bench press. By doing so, he had blasted a few holes in some key heart valves.

What is surprising is how much Henry cared.

I had spent so much time being terrified of Danny that I had not stopped to examine the emotional side of their relationship: The effete fashionista and the street-fighting, fist-pumping hustler . . . were they really in love?

When Henry came back from visiting Danny's family, I made him a cup of Kukicha twig tea and asked him how he was doing. He got teary and changed the subject.

when bossy bitches roamed the earth

BEFRIEND A HUNGARIAN gypsy and buy up all her shawls. Have a seamstress make them into tango dresses for you to wear to your parent-teacher meetings. It's time to *make an impression!*

Soak your feet in molten molasses. The hotter the temperature, the more beautiful the pedicure.

Do not even think of leaving the house this season unless you are wearing a puce-colored leotard and a scalloped zebra cape.

You would be mad not to dye all your underwear cerise.

It's all about the carelessness of a bare leg. Donate all your silk stockings to the Carmelite nuns, now!

Cardigans must be worn back to front . . . always! In fact, everything must be worn front to back, even your husband's Y-fronts. You must insist upon it or suffer the unstylish consequences.

More than anything else in the entire world, you need a

canary yellow Mongolian lamb evening muff. The fluffier the better.

Cut up your old ball gowns, sew them into ascots and give them to all your male friends. Save one for that homeless man who lives in a cardboard box near your house. There's no reason why he should be deprived of sartorial flourishes.

When will the women of America understand? A tambourine *is* an accessory! Carry one at all times.

BACK IN THE LAST CENTURY, back before the notion of empowerment gathered steam, back before we all turned against authority figures and began "doing our own thing," the fashion world was governed by an elite group of dictatorial maniacs. These tyrants felt duty bound to machine-gun the rest of the population with inspirational commands and bossy edicts. They told women to "think pink!" and to never picnic without a candelabra, to always use a coral ciggie holder, and to "banish the beige!"

Yes, Polly Mellen, I am talking about you.

Editor and visionary, La Mellen displayed no interest in prosaic dos and don'ts or prissy suburban etiquette. Fashion, for Polly, is, and has always been, a majestic, magical, mysterious galleon in full sail, and you would be INSANE not to hurl convention to the wind and jump on board.

While her reputation within the fashion world is the stuff of legend—in her decades-long career as a fashion editor, she collaborated with the greatest photographers of the twentieth century—she is perhaps best known for upstaging Isaac Mizrahi in what might be the most intriguing fashion movie of all time, namely *Unzipped*.

"Fussy finished," intones Mellen, silencing all further debate on the issue of simplicity versus ornamentation for the rest of eternity.

"Be careful of makeup. Be careful," says Mellen, sending a shiver of regret down the spine of anyone who has ever not been sufficiently wary of mascara or foundation and lived to tell the tale.

As her collaborations with Avedon and Bruce Weber et al can attest, Polly was always explosively hyperbolic and provocative. However, her creative flights of fancy are underpinned with a can-do practicality. Posture-perfect Polly is from the never-complain-never-explain school of life, advising women to "walk like a winner . . . do your crying at home."

Polly's enthusiasm for style is unbridled and unparalleled. I was present at shows where she excitedly clutched handfuls of skirt fabric as gals trotted down the runway, bringing the proceedings to a screeching halt. Sometimes Polly was so bowled over by a particular garment or model that she would be able to utter only one word, and that word was "chills."

I first encountered Polly in the mid-eighties. She blasted into the mayhem of a busy sportswear wholesale showroom. I had stopped by to visit a pal whose job was flogging these *schmattas* to the big department stores.

"Polly's here!" hissed the fashion pack, and it hid behind its collective lacquered Ming Dynasty fan. Chills.

Polly and her gaggle of assistants caused an immediate frisson of excitement. It was like a scene from William Klein's genius surrealist fashion fantasy, *Qui Étes-Vous, Polly Maggoo?* with Lady Mellen in the role of the editor, the lady who declares, *"Vous avez recréer la femme!"* to the stunned designer.

Upon sighting the racks of sporty commercial samples, Ms. Mellen froze in the doorway. Her eyebrows shot up in the air and she gasped audibly. All eyes swiveled toward Polly. We waited for her to speak.

"Something is happening!" she said, sniffing the air like a panther seeking out a gazelle for lunch.

"*Something* is definitely happening . . . right here!"

We all knew Polly was intuitive, but who knew she could suss out genius without even coming within twenty feet of the clothing in question?

She turned and addressed her posse.

"Something *is* happening here. Mark my words. And you, and you, and you must stay here until you find out exactly what it is," she said, pivoting on her heels and abandoning her bewildered assistants.

"DO NOT LEAVE!"

The assistants looked at one another like a bunch of startled ferrets for about five minutes. When they were sure Madam Polly was in the elevator, they slowly began to work their way through the racks of T-shirts and basic summer shift dresses.

Polly had clocked the simple nature of this particular fashion collection. Gotten the picture. Done it. Been there. She was too well brought up to simply about-face, so she instructed her assistants to go in search of a will-o'-the-wisp, a je ne sais quoi.

Insane, yes, but who knows? Maybe one of those anxious aco-lytes might actually find "something."

Though she could be serious, imperious and filled with fash-ion gravitas, Miss Mellen also loved a good chuckle. My favorite memory of Polly is sitting with her and Carolyn Murphy at the Met Ball—back in the last century, of course—critiquing the couture of the attendees while simultaneously counting the num-ber of times Donatella Versace and Kate Moss minced across the room for a potty break à deux.

Speaking of the Met . . . let's talk about the most fabulous fashion dictator who ever lived, the woman who mentored Polly. Yes—Diana Vreeland.

DV was a real empress's empress. Her mission was to liber-ate women from humdrum convention and propel them into a world of fantasy by using electrifying edicts filled with shock and awe.

Many of DV's bossy pronouncements were of the you'd-be-mad-not-to variety, though her most memorable style tips took the form of inspirational *suggestions*. Cunningly framed as ques-tions, these life-enhancing promptings were more powerful than if they had been simple direct commandments. I am referring to her famous "Why Don't You?" column in *Harper's Bazaar*.

Why don't you . . .

. . . waft a big bouquet about like a fairy wand?

. . . use a gigantic shell instead of a bucket to ice your cham-pagne?

. . . cover a big cork bulletin board in bright pink felt, band it with bamboo, and pin with colored thumbtacks all your various enthusiasms as your life varies from week to week?

. . . turn your old ermine coat into a bathrobe?

. . . paint a map of the world on all four walls of your boys' nursery so they won't grow up with a provincial point of view?

. . . tie black tulle bows on your wrists?

. . . remember that little girls and boys look divine in tiny green felt Tyrolean hats—the smaller the child, the longer the feather?

. . . wear violet velvet mittens with everything?

. . . have an elk-hide trunk for the back of your car? Hermès of Paris will make this.

. . . have a room done up in every shade of green? This will take months, years, to collect, but it will be delightful—a mélange of plants, green glass, green porcelains, and furniture covered in sad greens; gay greens; clear, faded and poison greens.

Vreeland was the primordial muck from which all subsequent bossy emperors and empresses emerged. She begat Polly and André Leon Talley and Carlyne Cerf de Dudzeele and Candy Pratts-Price and, yes, dare I say it—moi.

I consider myself fortunate to have worked for Empress Vreeland. It was during her tenure at the Metropolitan Museum Costume Institute. I was hired by DV in 1985 to design the displays for a Met exhibit titled *Costumes of Royal India* and spent four sequin-encrusted months szhooshing bejeweled saris onto mannequins. And, yes, there was no shortage of pink ones. (Vreeland once famously declared, "Pink *is* the navy blue of India.")

I have many happy memories of this period.

I remember Vreeland, who was allegedly color-blind, forcing the painters to repaint the walls ad nauseam until they got the "correct" shade. This persnickety obsession even extended to the gift shop: "Wrong! Not THAT gray. I want the gray of QUAKERS!" The painting and repainting went on for weeks. By the end of the show, there was so much paint clogging the walls that they had to cover them with fresh Sheetrock for the next exhibit.

I remember DV engaged in a cold war with the conservation department. Obeying the stringent guidelines issued by the teams of lab-coat-wearing, white-gloved conservation ladies was not in the Vreeland wheelhouse. Though much of the Met fashion archive was antique and disintegrating, Vreeland loved nothing more than to drag an eighteenth-century coat out of its tissue-paper coffin and—*quelle horreur!*—try it on for size! She would then strike period-appropriate attitudes. As far as the conservation department ladies were concerned, this was the equivalent of throwing acid at the *Mona Lisa*.

I remember Vreeland's office, with its blood-red walls and leopard carpet. The cork board behind her desk was smothered with inspirational photos: Maria Callas screaming, Veruschka vamping, Nijinsky leaping. DV was a cultivated broad whose life spanned most of the twentieth century. She had met everyone from Buffalo Bill to Brigitte Bardot. (She once insightfully observed that Brigitte's lips "made Mick Jagger's lips *possible*.")

I remember Vreeland's personal style. She wore kabuki-style rouge on her ears and massive black rosettes on her shoes. Her nuanced look was a palimpsest of all her previous incarnations: a thirties hairdo, a fifties manicure, a sixties go-go boot. There's a lesson there for us all: If something suits you, hang on to it and drag it with you into the next decade.

My mother did the same thing. In the 1940s she adopted a

Bette Davis pompadour (circa *Now, Voyager*) and the very same hairdo adorned her head when we buried her forty years later. There was a brief moment in the sixties when she experimented with a trendy updo of tunnel curls, accented with dangly earrings. She came home from the hairdresser, took one look in the mirror and declared, "I look like a tart." She then stuck her head under the kitchen faucet and reconstructed her *Voyager* pompadour.

I remember how much Vreeland loved Bill Cunningham. DV was convinced that every Met costume installation needed to have a contribution from the bicycle-riding photographer-milliner-fashion sage. On the occasion of the Royal India show, I was instructed to leave space for a white peacock in one of my maharajah dioramas. Bill, an amateur taxidermist, had promised DV that he would deliver a specimen, stuffed and preening, in time for the opening.

Days passed. The clock ticked. No peacock. I stared anxiously at the empty space, already spotlighted, which awaited the arrival of Bill's bird.

On the last day of the installation Bill careened into the parking lot on his bicycle. On the handlebars was a large object in a trash bag. Yes, it was Mr. Peacock. Hugely relieved, I indicated the allotted space and left Bill to unwrap, fluff and install his creation. Returning half an hour later, I was greatly amused by what I saw.

Bill's bird was a real *mieskeit*, a total Marty Feldman of a peacock. It was a strangely unmajestic bird, an enigma, a mutant.

I asked Bill where he found this unpeacock.

"Oh, young fella, it's not a peacock. I was cycling through Central Park and I found a dead seagull, and I thought, *Perfect! For Diana's show!* So I took it home and stuffed it and added goose feathers and peacock feathers! Voilà!"

With a little careful lighting and judicious angling, Bill's seagull delivered a remarkably good impersonation of a regal peacock. There is yet another lesson for us all: When in doubt, make sure you are totally backlit.

More memories . . .

After the opening, I remember having dinner with DV at her apartment. This was the exquisite red-lacquered Park Avenue aerie which Billy Baldwin had created for Madame in response to her request for "a garden in hell." The living room was a decadent, fabulously overdecorated opium den. The walls and upholstery were a hallucinogenic sea of blazing red patterns and foliage. Every horizontal surface was jammed with objects: turtle shells, silver-dipped seashells, lacquered boxes, enamel snuff boxes. Vreeland was no stranger to the concept of the tablescape.

She smoked throughout the entire evening, clutching a ciggie in one hand and, in the other, a handheld buzzer which summoned her housekeeper. On this particular occasion, Vreeland seemed less than pleased with her staff. Apparently they were attempting to dilute her vodka. Like many women of her generation, DV had developed an impressively high tolerance for booze. Any sneaky attempts to minimize her intake were met with lots of frantic buzzing.

When the meal arrived, Vreeland took revenge on her vodka saboteurs.

"Euch!" she said, viewing the deliciously simple chicken-'n'-two-veggies platter with exquisite disdain. "Take it away and make it into sandwiches! And bring me a cup of borscht!"

I remember Vreeland's memorial. This was the mega A-list occasion when Richard Avedon pointedly lauded the old guard, Vreeland, and dissed the new arrival, Anna Wintour. (La Wintour had recently arrived at *Vogue* and had earned Avedon's ire by cancelling his long-standing contract.)

I took my seat in a strange little angled pew. I looked up and gulped. I was seated facing Jackie Onassis, just three feet away. She was a longtime friend of DV's and had been the recipient of much fashion advice, most especially after becoming First Lady. The depth of their friendship was more than apparent during the memorial: Jackie O sobbed openly throughout. Afterward, I heard socialite Pat Buckley telling somebody, "Jackie always cries at funerals because she was not allowed to cry at Jack's."

Chills.

Vreeland got the send-off she deserved. She was the empress to end all empresses. With her mind-blowingly unconventional worldview, she understood that fashion was more than just smart dressing for rich ladies. She knew the importance of panache and eccentricity, and of adding a dash of vulgarity to the mix: "A little bad taste," she said, "is like a nice splash of paprika."

Where did all those dictatorial divas go? Do we have a Vreeland for the twenty-first century?

The truth is that the empress is, in the twenty-first century, as dead as the dodo. The world has changed. Gals no longer need provocation or liberating edicts from a crazy old broad who wore her hair in a jet-black helmet that resembled a chic beetle. Thanks to Vreeland and her ilk, they are already free.

Vreeland liberated women from the oppression of girdles and white gloves. She gave them a sense of creative possibilities. We live in the era of self-expression and rabid individuality which Vreeland dreamed about and helped create. Yes, there are status-obsessed real housewives who are conformist and dreary, but they pale in comparison to the hordes of liberated, groovy chicks and eccentric gals. If Vreeland were alive today, she would look at Ke$ha and Tavi and Nicki and Gaga and Florence and Gwen and Daphne and Riri and Tilda—and yes, even Miley and Kat von D.—with amusement and satisfaction. Mission accomplished.

tears for frocks

MY MATERNAL Irish grandfather may have had no teeth, no impulse control, and no money, but he did have one saving grace. He had a great way with words, and by a great way with words I mean to say that he had an impressive repertoire of jarring and unsavory expressions. And no matter how plastered he was, no matter how many vats of Guinness had gone down his gullet, no matter how irate or dégagé he was, Gramps never lost the ability to regurgitate one of his signature snappy phrases at exactly the right conversational juncture.

Unsurprisingly, many of these expressions centered around the word "arse." Examples include the following:

"That's a boil far from my arse."

"You know as much about [insert topic here] as my arse knows about snipe shooting." Example: "You know as much about the Panama Canal as my arse knows about snipe shooting."

"My arse in parsley!"

The latter expression was ol' Grampy's equivalent of "balderdash!" and was used when he had lost the inclination to continue an argument.

Then there were expressions which were utilized while dissecting a pal or an enemy in absentia. This was the "that bastard" group.

"That bastard has long pockets and short arms."

"That bastard would drink beer out of a shitey rag."

While many of his expressions focused on the less-than-positive attributes of the male species, women were by no means overlooked. If, for example, a drinking pal predeceased his wife then Grandpa might say, "That bastard preferred the boards," indicating that the gentleman in question found it preferable to be nailed into a wooden coffin and flung in the cold earth rather than continue cohabiting with his charmless harridan of a wife.

If the charmless harridan was prone to weeping, Grampy would shake his head, roll his eyes, swallow a mouthful of Guinness, exhale heartily and declare, "Auch! Her bladder is way too near her eyeballs."

Of all Grandpa's expressions, this gem concerning bladders and eyeballs is the one that has stayed with me. I call upon it with startling regularity. It has been far more useful than I would ever have imagined. During my life, I have frequently had occasion to speculate about the proximity of bladders and eyeballs. In my chosen milieu, there is no shortage of lachrymose females and males. Simply put, we fashion people cannot stop crying.

Before I entered the fashion asylum, I used to cry, but only very occasionally. I remember crying at the end of *Imitation of Life*, when Mahalia Jackson sings "Trouble of the World" at

Annie's funeral. By the time she was belting out "There'll be no more a-weepin' and a-wailin'," I was doing just that, right along with Sandra Dee and Lana Turner.

I cried when I first saw Doris Day sing "Secret Love" in *Calamity Jane*. There's Calam, all spiffed up in her western man drag, looking for all intents and purposes like an extremely attractive butch lesbian, singing her heart out about a secret love which "became impatient to be free." The next minute she's shouting it from the highest hill and even telling the golden daffodil. It's a beautiful hymnal homage to all the inverts throughout history who were forced to hide their proclivities and sit on their emotions.

Though prone to these occasional moments of sentimentality, I never thought my bladder was abnormally near my eyeballs. I never imagined that I would . . . Oh! The shame of it! . . . *cry at fashion shows*.

It all started in the late 1980s.

I was attending the European Collections for the first time. I was seated front row at Giorgio Armani. Though I never wore Armani clothing myself—that longer, drapey cut is a disaster for the altitudinally disadvantaged—I was barely able to contain my feelings of Euro-fizzy excitement. Images of a greige-linen-clad Richard Gere, futzing and primping his way through *American Gigolo*, spooled through my head. My anticipation reached orgasm level when I found myself seated directly opposite the legendary Elsa Klensch.

Elsa who?

Elsa Klensch is part of fashion history. She was the first fashion TV media icon. Back in the day, back before fashion had become a culturally central global obsession, back before *Sex and the City* and *Ugly Betty*, back before *Project Runway*, back when *Roseanne* was the most stylish show on TV, there was only one program dedicated to fashion. *One*. And Elsa Klensch was the host thereof.

Elsa's show was called *Style with Elsa Klensch*. With her glossy brunette bob and dramatically contour-blushed cheeks, the well-spoken Elsa was the absolute tits. Every Sunday morning hungover fashion addicts would set their alarm clocks and tune in to CNN to watch La Klensch's overview of the fashion scene, all delivered in her trademark Aussie posh-lady drawl.

"This week we're going to the home of Krizia designer Mariuccia Mandelli" became, in Elsa-speak, "Theese wick we're gee-owing to the heeome of Kreezia dezahner Meeyarryoocheeya Meendeellee."

Do not think for a moment that I am mocking her. Elsa was major. How major? The following brief digression will, hopefully, provide the answer to this question.

Back in the era of Elsa, I lived in one large room in lower Manhattan. Having grown up in a labyrinthine rooming house packed with batty relatives and lodgers—and one toilet—I had always fantasized about inhabiting one large, serene room. At an impressionable age I had seen the Agnès Varda movie titled *Cléo de 5 à 7*, about an actress who lives in one square white room. This culty gem became the blueprint for my future. I saw myself living a life of unconventional *nouvelle vague* abandon, just like the überchic heroine. Fantasy aside, a one-room pad always made sense to me. As Quentin Crisp once said, "I like living in one room and have never known what people do with the room they're not in."

Directly opposite my groovy miniloft was a Japanese restaurant which I patronized on a regular basis, as did many fashion folk. Among the dessert offerings was a wholesome concoction named "fruit crunch." Struggling, and failing, to pronounce the *r*'s, the Asian server would always refer to it as "fluit clunch." For me and my fashion pals, this was irresistible: we renamed it "Elsa Klunch." *That's* how mega Elsa was, back in the day.

"Two Elsa Klunches, please!"

It's a stupid story but it does illustrate just how iconic Elsa had become.

So there I was sitting opposite Ms. Fluit Klunch at the Giorgio Armani show, worshipping the magnificence of fashion's only TV pundit and feeling overwhelmed by my Elsa proximity.

The show begins.

The parade of cadaverous beauties starts to slither down the runway. The operatic music soars. There is an exquisite melancholy perfection to the unsmiling faces and the flawlessly tailored garments. The models appear hauntingly and gorgeously doomed, like Dominique Sanda in *The Conformist* or Charlotte Rampling in *The Damned*.

About halfway through the show, I look across at Elsa and I notice that her face is suddenly crumpling. Before long, a large mascara-streaked tear makes its way down her rouged face.

What gives?

Is her bladder too near her eyeballs?

"Maybe her TV show got cancelled," suggests an adjacent colleague.

"Maybe it's that time of the month," conjectures a more sympathetic voice.

I do not say anything, for I find, much to my surprise, that I too have become teary.

When I get outside into the cold, polluted light of the Milanese winter, I suddenly feel bizarre and ridiculous. What on earth had come over me? I am so ashamed. Whatever would grumpy, super-butch, toothless Gramps have made of his effete grandchild, blubbering at a fashion show? Clearly my bladder must have migrated to within a millimeter of my eyeballs.

As more shows unfurled, this illogical weeping reoccurred. I moistened at Moschino. I grieved at Givenchy. If there was a bridal finale, forget about it, especially if the no-longer-in-the-first-flush-of-youth designer accompanied the bride.

And I was by no means the only one. At Yves Saint Laurent *les clients*, rows and rows of them, all clutched their *mouchoirs* as Monsieur Saint Laurent took his bows.

Another and much more important digression: Let's take a moment to talk about *les clients*.

Back in the day, *les clients* had pride of place at every fashion show. The most important women in the room were the loyal chicks who opened their handbags and actually purchased the clothes . . . at full retail, I might add! At some point in the nineties, designers decided that the paying clients were less important than bold-faced notables and entertainment celebrities. So the broads who paid full price were displaced by the freebie-demanding generation of A-, B-, and J-listers.

Unfair and illogical, right?

The high-fashion world turned into a gifting suite, a place

where beautiful clothes are given or loaned to the only people who can afford them . . . and actually *need* them.

And what of *les clients*?

Fortunately there are still women who pay full retail. In my current role as Creative Ambassador at Barneys, I get to travel to the stores and meet these chicks . . . and pay homage to them. In a world where more and more gals are looking for a "press discount" or a "loaner," the women who are happy and willing to pay full retail are the fashion equivalent of angel investors. If there were any justice in the world, they would be back front and center at every fashion show.

Off the soapbox and back to my bladder.

As I flew home after that first trip, I reflected upon my emotional volatility. What had brought my bladder into such close proximity to my eyeballs? And why were so many other people crying too? Was it group hysteria?

Upon reflection, I realized that what I had experienced was peculiar to La Mode. It is a runway-specific emotion. Let's call it *fashion verklempt*.

Over the years I have been able to observe the *fashion verklempt* phenomenon repeatedly, both in myself and others. I have tried without success to isolate the triggers for these tear-jerking moments.

Jetlag is definitely a factor. I can't recall ever having cried during the New York fashion shows, most of which take place within shrieking distance of my abode.

Music is a factor. Whether anthemic or operatic, cheerfully folksy or grungily forlorn, there are many genres which can precipitate the *fashion verklempt* phenomenon.

In certain specific instances, the fashion-show soundtrack has had the effect of making me cry . . . with laughter. Two occasions spring to mind.

In the early nineties I was sitting at the Chanel show. These were startling, fabulously frenetic affairs. Glamazons like Christy, Linda, Cindy, Naomi, Marpessa, Veronica and Tatiana careened up and down the runways in chaotic, laughing, posing, vamping groups. This was before the grim mechanical goose-stepping trend which now dominates every runway show. (A journalist recently asked me if I thought the runway models of the future would be robots rather than humans. "You clearly have not been to a fashion show in a while," I replied, adding, "The Cylons are already here.")

The Chanel soundtrack consisted, in this particular instance, of mashed-up, sampled music clearly put together by somebody with great flair but a limited knowledge of English. I base this conclusion on the fact that the music-meister elected to incorporate a pornographically abrasive rant. It was a dirty ditty sung by Marianne Faithfull and titled "Why D'Ya Do It?"

Watching the English speakers in attendance—including the UK and American press—wincing repeatedly as Marianne Faithfull railed at her lover about some chick with "cobwebs up her fanny" and demanded to know why he "spit on her snatch" was an exquisitely amusing *Ab Fab* moment.

A similar *folie musicale* occurred at a men's Armani show around the same time. The DJ decided to sample the soundtrack of a Derek Jarman movie. The phrase "rosy-cheeked choirboys in semen-stained cassocks" played over and over again as the handsome besuited young lads walked the runway. While the

Asian contingents respectfully watched the show with inscrutable expressions on their faces, we English speakers wept with mirth.

Speaking of choirboys: There was one memorable occasion when I totally lost it. My bladder and my eyeballs finally merged. It happened at a late-nineties Junya Watanabe show. The soundtrack was supplied by a pink-cheeked prepubescent English choirboy. Live and in person, the young lad sang hauntingly beautiful Elizabethan songs—a cappella, no mike—while the avant-garde Watanabe creations floated past. There was something overwhelmingly touching about his earnestness, and about that impossibly perfect voice which was just months away from cracking and disappearing into the mists of time. Blub. Blub.

The biggest group weep fest—the wailing wall of the *fashion verklempt*—occurred at the 1989 Romeo Gigli show. Mr. Gigli was one of the most influential fashion designers of the late twentieth century. He popularized a whole new wrappy way of dressing women. His color palate—dusky maroon, Moroccan apricot, cat-poo brown and acid green—had such far-reaching influence that even the famous Gap pocket T's began to be hued accordingly. He introduced nifty suit cuts, flat-front narrow pants, and sumptuous colors and fabrics for men. Like Christian Lacroix, he burned very bright and made a huge impact.

Back to the weep fest.

The Carrousel du Louvre was filled with a soaring Verdi soundtrack. The models wore majestic robes in rich browns and burgundys. The entire collection was inspired by the mosaics of Ravenna depicting the wild and mysterious Empress

Theodora of Byzantium. The gals were festooned with necklaces made from oversize handblown Murano glass beads. Each wrapped and draped outfit was more stately than the next. The presentation was impressive, so impressive that, come the finale, the audience was delivering a standing ovation and weeping, weeping, weeping. Even the hard-boiled retailers were *fashion verklempt*.

And the bladder fest continues . . .

Even as I write, I am hearing reports of front-row editors sobbing at the beauty of the Haider Ackermann fall collection. Ditto Raf Simons. His dénoument at maison Jil Sander sent more than a few fashion insiders lurching for their Kleenex.

What would toothless Grampy say about all this? Would he declare it all to be a boil far from his arse? Would he denounce us for our frivolous way of life and condemn us all to drink beer out of shitey rags?

Who cares! So what if we are all a bunch of *verklempt* nellies! So what if our bladders are located too near our eyeballs. At least we have all our own teeth . . . or most of them.

suzy menkes's
saucisson

SUZY MENKES'S ROCKABILLY pompadour hairdo has been through a lot. It has seen presidents come and go. It has seen shoulder pads go in and out and then come rushing back in again. Ditto platform shoes, bustiers, jewel tones and tiaras. It has seen Jil Sander leave her company and return years later in triumph. It has seen the shock of the new and the tedium of the greige. It has seen models falling off runways and designers falling off the wagon. That legendary glamorous roll of coiffure has seen it all, the great and the good, the prosaic and the avant-garde, the power and the glory, the naked and the damned. If it could only talk . . .

If Suzy Menkes's hairdo could talk, it would tell tales of glamour and jubilation, of torn seams and broken dreams. One day I hope to get some alone time with Suzy Menkes's sausage. I am sure that Suzy will let it go out for a playdate with me. I like to think that she would trust me to take good care of her signature coiffure.

While Suzy stays at home, banging out more of her brilliant fashion commentary—she is *the* most insightful, knowledgeable fashion commentator of our age—we, the sausage and I, will ensconce ourselves in the corner of a quiet bar on the Rive Gauche. I will ply the sausage with absinthe and I won't stop until it has coughed up all its gothic secrets and mysterious memories. Suzy has always been very discreet, but I am sure her sausage will spill the beans.

I might start by asking the sausage about a near-death experience which happened back in the early nineties. I remember it well. It was a where-were-you-when moment. I was there. I witnessed the deluge and lived to tell the tale.

THE STORY I am about to relate takes place long ago, before the arrival of the Bryant Park tents. Fashion designers were still showing their collections in their hot, stuffy, carpeted showrooms. Another option: if you didn't have a large enough showroom then you went off-site. On this particular occasion, Michael Kors went off-site, off-Broadway and quite, for him and for the time, Euro avant-garde. He chose to show his collection in a crumbling industrial space.

From my seat I can see Suzy and her sausage. They are seated next to Anna Wintour and her bob. I am parked in the second row on the retail side of the runway. As fate would have it, this second-row *placement* turned out to be a lifesaver . . . but let's not get ahead of ourselves.

I am excited to see Michael's collection. He had shared little tidbits of inspiration over the previous summer. Michael and

I are beach neighbors in Fire Island Pines. He rents an ocean-front glam palace with loungers and tinkling glasses filled with Pimm's. In keeping with his branding commitment to jet-set glamour, there are ramparts of thirsty white towels, heaps of squishy floor pillows, aerosol sunblockers and lashings of international fashion magazines.

I am in an adjacent house, or rather I am under an adjacent house. My pal Steven Johanknecht—aka Chiclet—and I have snagged what might just be the deal of the century. For a negligible rent, we are beachfront and Kors adjacent. The only downside: We are in a single, stiflingly hot, windowless room in the basement. The décor? Ours looks like the kind of place where a serial killer would keep his victims before murdering and flaying them. A black vinyl foldout couch and a wall of gold-veined mirror tiles provide the only decorative flourishes. Ike Turner meets Sid Vicious. In no time we learn to unpeel each other from the couch. This action is accompanied by a comforting coming-unstuck sound. While Michael is rocking jet-set glamour, we are within shrieking distance and living in a sub-trailer-park hovel. I would call it "grunge" except grunge has not yet been invented. So I will just go with "gnarly."

For obvious reasons, we spend a great deal of time chez Kors, lolling on the massive architectural deck and gossiping with the always entertaining MK. Like Chiclet and me, Michael loves to dissect the sociology and anthropology of the strange time warp that is Fire Island Pines. In many regards, nothing has changed since the disco seventies. One feels as if one is about to be photographed for a cheesy spread in *After Dark* magazine. Old-school queens in caftans waft down the teensy boardwalk clutching a cocktail in one hand and a poodle in the other. The music at the Pavilion's tea dance is a decade old and straight out of the cliché end of the Studio 54 disco canon. We find this to be pathos drenched but also rather delightful.

Among Michael's disco faves is a classic titled "Use It Up and Wear It Out" by Odyssey. The chorus may well be familiar to readers *d'un certain âge*.

"One two three . . . shake your body down."

So enamored is Michael of this smokin' hot dance ditty of yesteryear that he elected to incorporate it into the soundtrack of his upcoming show.

Which brings us back to the gritty space and Suzy's *saucisson*.

So there I am, perched in my second-row seat, jonesing, not just for the clothes but also for the soundtrack. The show begins and, sure enough, in no time at all we hit the opening bars of "Use It Up and Wear It Out." It is undeniably catchy. The throbbing music gets Suzy's toe tapping. I swear I can see her luscious hair-roll pulsing in time to the music.

Out walks Gauguin-esque beauty Anna Bayle. At this point in the song, we are just about to hit the first "one two three."

The volume increases dramatically. In my mind, I can see Michael backstage vigorously jiggling a coat hanger in an upward motion, indicating to his sound guy that this is the moment to *blow the lid off* and TURN THE MOTHER OUT!

Up goes the volume . . .

and down comes the ceiling.

As the phrase "shake your body down" reaches my ears, the spectacle in front of me goes into slow motion. Large slices of concrete and plaster descend onto the runway. Shake your body down has shaken the ceiling down onto the heads of the most important people in the fashion industry. A cloud of dust and debris has engulfed the first row.

In amongst the screams and the sound of falling debris, I hear a familiar male voice yelling, "Cut the disco!"

As the dust clears and the music finally dies, a poignant vignette emerges. There is Anna Wintour, her signature bob intact but dusted with white powder in the manner of an eighteenth-century princess at Versailles, and she is leaning over Suzy Menkes. In a kind and caring and meticulous manner she is extracting lumps of plaster, which have lodged themselves in, on, and behind Suzy's hairdo.

Post-traumatic stress has erased much of what happened subsequently. But I do remember the fashion flock tiptoeing out of the industrial space so as not to dislodge any more debris. Within hours, Suzy was back in the front row doggedly covering the next show.

From whence cometh this resilience? What engenders this kind of passionate commitment to La Mode?

I feel sure that if I could just have some face time with Suzy's legendary *saucisson*, he/she/it could help me to get inside Suzy's head, and all would be revealed.

postscript Michael remembers: "When I first heard the boom from backstage, I thought it was gunfire. Anna Bayle came off the runway screaming that the ceiling had fallen and hit Suzy Menkes. I rushed out from backstage to make sure everyone was okay. We swept up the mess, turned down the music to inaudible and continued the show. I couldn't believe Suzy and everyone stayed, but fashion folks are a strong group. In that best Broadway phrasing, I always wanted my collections to bring down the house—but not so literally."

Suzy remembers: "My memory of the whole thing is that Eleanor Lambert, aged ninety-something, was much smarter than I was and got up and scuttled out as the first piece of plaster fell. (You don't get to ninety-something for nothing.) I ask myself why I never sued the good Kors. Brits just don't!"

rei
kawakubo's
pasties

JAPAN IS A FREAKY SCENE. It's a lethal combo of beauty and perversity. It's schoolgirl panties sold in vending machines. It's a silk obi woven by a two-thousand-year-old toothless crone from threads produced by hermaphroditic silkworms and then wound so tightly around your middle that your internal organs keep threatening to come flying out of your orifices.

Japan is a giant watermelon scooped out and filled with ice so that one single ridiculously tiny morsel of haute couture sashimi can rest in splendor on the top. Japan is also a square watermelon, imprisoned in a box, screaming to be round, but forced to be cube shaped for unspecified aesthetic reasons.

It's about going to restaurants with your nearest and dearest, and then not uttering a single word of conversation for hours, but remaining quite happy and content in your silence. And when the food is plonked in front of you, it's about obsessively documenting it with your phone.

It's about sitting in a pachinko parlor for weeks at a time without ever stopping to pee or eat or sleep while stuffing fistfuls of teensy ball bearings into those mysterious machines, and wearing a blank expression which suggests that you are blissfully but inexplicably unaware of the hideous eardrum-destroying cacophony inside said parlor.

In the eighties I traveled to Japan with a female colleague who was wearing a modest scoop-neck dress. The man who met us at the airport stared at her barely visible cleavage and said, "Soon may I have some milk to drink please, Mommy?" He then put on little white Mickey Mouse gloves and drove us to our hotel.

On the same trip I wandered into a Shinjuku porn store. I wasn't looking for kicks. It was more of a Margaret Mead kind of a thing. The exhausted and wildly unhot store proprietor exhaled his ciggie and gave me a deadpan guide to his emporium of erotica.

"Old lady porn here. Schoolgirl porn there. Fat, ugly businessman porn under here. What you want?"

Helpful service, along with beauty and perversity, is also very much part of the Japanese scene. And then there's fashion . . .

On a more recent trip to Tokyo I saw about fifty girls standing outside Shibuya Station, each dressed up like a Madame Alexander doll, ringlets, starched crinolines, graphic circles of rouge on the cheeks, Victorian lace-up ankle booties, frilly bloomers, the whole megillah. I was told that these indigenous kooksters refer to this particular style as Gottic Rorita. Translation: Gothic Lolita.

Bonnets aside, the most noteworthy thing about these gals was that they were trying to look nonchalant, and they were succeeding. There is something deeply perverse about dragging yourself up as a life-size Madame Alexander doll and then walking about in public as if you were wearing slacks and a simple sweater.

"I dress like oversize doll for no reason—not big deal" their blank expressions seemed to say.

I am guessing about the Gottic Rorita interior monologue. Maybe there is no introspection. Maybe there is just the sound of an old-fashioned musical jewelry box? Tinkle. Tinkle. Tinkle. In Japan you are forced to rely on guesswork because nobody speaks much. This is a good thing. It's a *sugoi* thing. The annoying Western compulsion to overcommunicate does not seem to have impacted the land of the Gottic Rorita. This absence of chatty badinage allows one to spend many blissful hours lost in creative speculation.

Lest I sound disrespectful, let me say for the record that I am in love with Japan. I have traveled there more times than I can remember and always found it insanely life enhancing in every aspect, especially the visual stuff. All of my creative idols are Japs: Yohji Yamamoto, Yayoi Kusama, Araki, Tomita, Tamasaburo Bando, Issey Miyake, Eiko Ishioka, Junya Watanabe, and, at the top of this list, Miss Rei Kawakubo.

Rei, pronounced Ray, is the reigning enigma of global fashion. Nobody knows if she is a bitch or an angel or a psycho. One thing is for sure: she is an object of fascination. With her rigorous black wardrobe and her blunt-cut hair framing her inscrutable face, Rei is a true icon. Deservedly so. Rei is one of the most influential fashion creators of all time, up there with Madame Vionnet, Coco Chanel, Azzedine Alaïa and Yves Saint Laurent.

John Waters has a long-standing obsession with Rei and has described her thus: "She is locked in a self-imposed deconstructed cell, like the Saint Teresa of fashion, massacring hemlines for next season's no-dimensional outfits that will be mocked, brilliantly reviewed and worn by the brave."

The legend of Rei—and her designer label, Comme des Garçons—results from the fact that she is supremely talented but also mute. During her half-century-plus career, Rei has mostly kept her trap shut, even during interviews. Kawakubo-san is famous for her ability to ignore quotidian questions. This can be very nerve-racking. Any journalist proposing to interrogate Rei would be well advised to wear adult diapers. Rei has more patience than you. She can weather a spaghetti western standoff for much longer than any bubbly reporter.

An intrepid pal once decided he would be the one to break through the wall of inscrutability. He would be the guy to warm her up and ignite the Chatty Cathy persona that he felt sure must lurk within.

He kicked things off with a real crowd pleaser.

"Have you ever thought about doing a line of children's clothing?"

A Comme des Garçons aide embarked on a painstaking translation while Rei stared straight ahead through black Ray-Bans. Silence followed the painstaking translation of the dorky question. Rei stared at my pal. My pal's butthole slowly began to shrivel. Rather than admit defeat and face the agonizing humiliation of moving on to the next question, he gave it another whirl.

"Children's clothing by Comme des Garçons?" bubbled my anxious friend, adding, "How fabulous would that be?"

Another painstaking translation followed by another excruciating silence.

"Whaddya think? Children? Clothing?"

My pal was starting to disintegrate and to sweat and to seriously understand the appeal of hari-kari.

The translator gave up and stared at Rei. Rei stared at my pal. Finally Rei elected to put them both out of their misery.

She spoke in English.

"I don't like children."

I consider myself something of an expert on Comme des Garçons, or CDG as we in the business refer to the company Rei founded in 1969. I have observed and displayed her collections since the early eighties and have attended many of her shows. I have touched the merch, the artfully constructed holes, the boiled wool, the raw seams, the fungal padding. When she designed costumes for Merce Cunningham, I cheered from the front row. When she was honored with a retrospective at the Fashion Institute of Technology, I was first in line.

On this latter occasion, the CDG archive was exhibited on clusters of strange, grim, gray cardboard mannequins. The effect was jarring and Orwellian. After the exhibit was dismantled, I called FIT and begged to borrow these grim figures for an installation at Barneys honoring Rei. FIT obliged and we trucked them down Seventh Avenue to the old Barneys, where they were immediately installed in the windows. Once the vignettes were completed, I took pictures and sent them to Rei. Her response was swift and dramatic. She immediately recalled her gray cardboard dollies to Japan, where they were fed into some kind of massive Dr. No granulating machine. After the dollycaust, it was explained to me that Rei had created these mannequins for the FIT exhibit and could not tolerate their use in any other context. Hello dolly. Good-bye dolly.

Speaking of granulations: For years it was rumored that Rei was in the habit of feeding last season's clothing into a giant incinerator. She could not endure the idea of unsold CDG items languishing at Forever 21 or Loehmann's alongside a bunch of conventional schlock. Better to immolate an asymmetrical blouse than to have it end up on a rolling rack next to a naff Seventh Avenue polyester patio gown.

Putting aside all the fables and legends, the most noteworthy thing about the Kawakubo oeuvre is the brilliance thereof. Rei is an undisputed genius whose influence is immeasurable. This is exemplified by the fact that her designs never go out of fashion: despite being so daringly experimental, Ms. Kawakubo's creations remain immune to the passage of time. Comme des Garçons never dies. CDG garments remain timelessly avant-garde, cool, and groovy.

During her long career, Rei has applied her genius to many areas of design, including accessories and furniture . . . and perfume.

In 1995, Rei introduced her first Comme des Garçons fragrance. Barneys was selected as the launching partner. I vividly remember the planning meeting at the Paris showroom with Rei and her South African–born husband, Adrian. Every aspect of this strange new product was riddled with Kawakuboian perversity.

The bottle was flat. It lay in the palm of your hand like a molded-glass river rock. Forget about ever getting it to stand up in your medicine cabinet. Forget about lining it up next to your bottles of White Diamonds or Jontue.

Then there was the color. The Comme des Garçons fragrance was a startling and challenging shade of yellow. Think about what you see when you take a whiz after you have overdone the vitamin B. Yes, *that* particular shade.

When describing the scent itself—and this might just be the most perverse bit of Japanobilia I have ever encountered—Rei went *inorganic*. Just when everyone else in the entire universe was going headlong down the sustainable, lesbian-certified, re-cycled, locavore, übercrunchy organic rabbit hole, Rei went in the totally opposite direction.

And what, precisely, were these inorganic top notes, middle notes and base notes?

According to Rei, they were electricity, granite and alumi-num. Who doesn't want to smell like an office park? (The ingre-dients are actually rose, cardamom, cedar, etc., etc., but Rei, for some deeply perverse reason, chose to promote the idea of an inorganic concept.)

The international CDG perfume launch started in Paris, around the pool at the Ritz. While synchronized gals in black swimsuits thrashed up and down, we guests made polite chit-chat. As per Rei, the décor of the party consisted of large trans-parent plastic bags filled with the yellow perfume. Bold, brave and vaguely obscene, they resembled mastodon-size bags of urine.

The Paris launch was a huge success. New York followed, as

did more colostomy bags. Fortunately none of them broke. By the time we got to Los Angeles, the concept no longer struck me as peculiar or jarring. "We need more giant colostomy bags," I instructed the L.A. display team as we prepared for Rei's fête, matter-of-factly adding, "Let's put a couple of biggies by the entrance and hit them with a yellow spotlight. Thanks, luvvies!"

To say that Rei Kawakubo appeared a little out of place in Beverly Hills would be a colossal understatement. While she has always looked right at home in a concrete bunker or next to a defunct nuclear reactor, when she wandered onto Rodeo Drive, she suddenly seemed like a space alien. The man-pleasing bimbo culture, the face-lifted superficiality and the fake tans all conspired to give Rei the appearance of a freaky *manga* cult leader.

The L.A. launch party was noteworthy for the following reason: I had sent an invite to photographer William Claxton and his wife, Peggy Moffitt, muse and collaborator to the late Rudi Gernreich. Peggy arrived in full-on futuristic vintage Gernreich drag, complete with Sassoon bowl cut and forty billion false eyelashes. There was a frisson between the two women. Rei seemed almost flirtatious. Having introduced them, I got quite excited about the notion of a clandestine lesbian affair between the two. A decade later Rei embarked on a platonic collaboration with La Moffitt. CDG T-shirts bearing images of Peggy's face became the must-have item of the season. Score a yenta brownie point for me.

Harry Dean Stanton came. The melancholy-looking actor had walked in Rei's men's shows—Rei has a history of casting improbable males for her presentations—and wanted to pay his respects.

And then the grand voilà! An unscheduled celebrity appearance of massive, pressworthy proportions.

Kato Kaelin crashed Rei's party.

The perfume launch occurred during the O. J. Simpson trial and Kato Kaelin, having recently given his rambling testimony, was the most recognizable face on the planet.

Kato had been lurking in the pool house on the night that O. J. had, allegedly, murdered his wife, Nicole Brown Simpson, and her unlucky visitor, Ron Goldman. Mr. Kaelin's abundant sun-bleached tresses and douche-bag good looks had made him an instant media star. There was a force field around the charming-but-sleazy Kato. As soon as he entered the store, the paparazzi began falling over the large yellow bags of perfume, trying to get a few words with him.

I tried explaining to Rei that a very important celebrity had just arrived. Distilling the broad strokes of the trial of the century into simple, coherent party chat was an impossible task. Rei stared straight ahead and nodded. A little smile upturned the corners of her mouth, suggesting that she was seriously considering casting him for the next men's show.

The après-fête dinner was held at Chasen's, a Hollywood classic and Liz Taylor's fave chili joint. Rei seemed to dig the old-school Hollywood vibe and the red Naugahyde booths. Was she envisioning an entire collection of padded trepunto rubber clothing in homage to the Chasen's banquettes?

She also fixated on the prevalence of toupee-wearing older dudes who were dining at adjacent tables with their busty, much younger wives. When, decades later, her male models wore strange little Brillo-pad wigs, I could not help but think that Rei was referencing the superannuated silver geezers of Chasen's with their artfully glued Sy Sperling rugs.

"What shall I do with Rei tomorrow?" asked Mickey, one of Kawakubo-san's trusted female minders. Rei had an entirely blank schedule the next day and a somewhat nervous Mickey was charged with identifying the local points of interest. She enlisted my help because she knew that I had spent a lot of time in Hollywood in the sleazy seventies and the early eighties.

I understood Mickey's anxiety. Where could one possibly send her? My mind reeled. Knott's Berry Farm seemed all wrong, and it was hard to imagine her enjoying the shark attack or the *Psycho* house at Universal Studios. Disneyland? Apparently she had already visited the one near Paris and had not cracked a smile. Surfing in Malibu? Bird-watching in Will Rogers State Park? What would inspire and stimulate the brain of the most creative woman in fashion? How do you recommend some dopey sightseeing opportunity and not look like an idiot? How do you solve a problem like Maria?

Eventually I had an epiphany.

I quickly scrawled a list of destinations onto the back of a Chasen's napkin. The next day I flew back to New York City. I picked up the pieces and moved on with my life.

FIFTEEN YEARS LATER I found myself twiddling my thumbs in the lobby of a Parisian hotel. The men's designer collections were about to unfurl. I had flown in on the red-eye and arrived too early for check-in. I sat on a squishy couch and began to nod off. A discreet trickle of drool began to edge its way down the front of my chocolate brown velvet traveling ensemble.

I was roused by the impact of a body squishing down next to me. I opened my bleary eyes and saw a pretty Asian gal. After peering at me a couple of times, she identified herself. It was the aforementioned Mickey. She was now running her own PR company and had come to Paris to oversee the press and *placement* of her top clients.

"Remember when we were all in L.A. for the perfume launch and you gave me an itinerary for Rei?"

I trawled back through my mental archives. As I hastily dabbed away my drool, my memories began to coalesce. I remembered the yellow colostomy bags and I remembered Kato Kaelin. But I had forgotten the details of my recommended itinerary. Where had I sent her?

Mickey filled me in.

As per my strict instructions, Mickey and Rei had started their day at Frederick's of Hollywood on Hollywood Boulevard. Keep in mind that this tour took place before Hollywood was gentrified and commercialized. Back then it was a dead zone of hairnet-wearing cholos, hookers, dope fiends, wild-eyed runaways and . . . drumroll . . . stripper shops. In an effort to deliver a truly authentic experience, I had plunged Rei into the bowels of sleazy mid-twentieth-century stripper culture, or what was left of it. The last gasp of burlesque was clinging to Hollywood Boulevard and, courtesy of me, Rei was up to her neck in it.

According to Mickey, Rei spent over an hour in Frederick's

examining—and intermittently purchasing!—cone bras, assless hostess skirts, crotchless knickers and edible panties. After Frederick's, the two gals made their way east in search of Playmates, one of the most fascinating sleazetiques ever to have plied its trade on Hollywood Boulevard. Massive and dirt cheap, Playmates was the store for supervixens and hookers who were too broke and down on their slingbacks to shop at Frederick's. This was *the* place to pick up a well-priced dental-floss bathing suit or a pair of those one-legged skintight slacks that are like a panty on one side and a complete slack leg on the other. And then there was the bargain basement.

The hangar-size Playmates cellar was a thing of wonder. Back when I lived down the street at the Fontenoy on Whitley Street and Yucca, I was a frequent rummager. I would spend hours looking through the boxes of supersize brassieres, over-the-shoulder boulder holders and sleazy peignoirs. Among my greatest finds of yore: a leopard velour swimsuit (think Jayne Mansfield's husband Mickey Hargitay); a midriff-bearing, striped-toweling pop-over which screamed Sal Mineo; and a *sauvage* John-Travolta-in-*Staying-Alive* fake chamois mankini.

As Mickey and I sipped our tea and recalled Rei's Hollywood outing, I could not help but cringingly reflect upon the preposterousness of sending the reigning queen of the avant-garde to truffle for inspiration in the bargain basement of a G-string and pastie store.

"What on earth did Rei make of it all?"

According to Mickey, Rei had gone into an intense, unblinking fugue state. With an archaeologist's ardor, she had poked through the endless bins and boxes of skimpy foundation garments, bejeweled brassieres and shop-soiled posing pouches and totally lost track of time. No garment was left untouched. They were there for *hours*.

When I heard that Rei had followed my suggestions with such commitment, I felt a tsunami of satisfaction. It was the opposite of asking her a question and having her not answer. I felt as if I had somehow communicated directly with her extraordinarily creative brain, and that this was the closest I might ever get to a hug.

balenciaga could sew with either hand

AT SOME POINT in the early seventies, as I flicked a feather duster over sunburst wall-mounted clocks, brass carriage clocks, booming grandfather clocks and those depressing rows of moc-croc travel alarms, I was compelled to ask myself a truly heavy question: *Is this how I am destined to spend the rest of my fucking life? Is this my lot?*

Cuckoo! Cuckoo! Cuckoo!

After graduating college, I had returned home to Reading, Berkshire, and taken a job selling clocks and watches at the local John Lewis department store. Though I did not realize it at the time, this was the starting point of my fashion odyssey.

How best to describe the general ambience of this retail institution?

Are You Being Served?

Whenever I catch an episode of that vintage Brit TV series, I feel like I'm watching a documentary, a painstakingly accurate record of my experience. The similarities between this absurdist sitcom and my own John Lewis tenure never fail to blow my mind: the frowsy merchandise displays, the faded gentility of the customers, the clunky prewar counter service, the bare-bones cafeteria, and, most important, the performances of the selling staff. Spewing saucy double entendres at one another and then suddenly acting all posh when a customer appeared, the John Lewis sales force was every bit as noteworthy as the characters in *A.Y.B.S.*

At John Lewis we had our Captain Peacocks and Mrs. Slocombs and our Mr. Humphries, and we never failed to approach customers with the phrase "Are you being served, sir?" We were not being even remotely ironic.

There was one big screaming difference. While *Are You Being Served?* had a deafening and continuous laugh track, my own real-life experience did not. Working in retail during one of the most blighted economic periods in British history turned out to be a grimly surreal endeavor. In the absence of moneyed customers, or any kind of customers, I occupied myself by keeping each timepiece fully wound and synchronized. A certain satisfaction came when, upon the hour, all the carriage clocks and cuckoos ejaculated and exploded into action, scaring the shit out of the few customers within earshot.

Things looked up when I was transferred to the luggage department. Getting away from the clocks—an unwanted reminder of the horribly relentless passing of time and the inevitable approach of death—was a huge relief. And there was something undeniably upbeat about travel goods. The sight of a spanking new avocado green (remember, we are talking about the early seventies) Samsonite Tourister with matching cosmetics case never failed to suggest that life elsewhere was full of possibilities.

And speaking of possibilities: I also found myself working alongside a certain tall, languid queen. This attenuated person was fun and amiable, but most important, this attenuated person had a special friend named Eric. The special friend named Eric was so special that he had made his way out of our hometown and struck gold. He was working—drumroll!—as a dress designer in London.

Eric did not design dresses, per se. His specialty was "missy separates." Missy separates were not to be sneezed at. Missy separates—tight sweaters, frilly blouses, tweedy skirts and slacks—were a huge business back then. Every young slag in Reading would somehow manage to scrape together the pennies to buy a "fab new top" or a "nifty skirt" to enhance her weekend pub crawls and nocturnal escapades.

Today, Reading is a barely recognizable gleaming beacon of reinvention. With a Premier League soccer team and masses of corporate investors such as Oracle setting up shop, Reading has never seemed more foofy and fabulous. Quel contrast! Back in my day, Reading was a slaggy, violent kind of town. On Saturday nights all the young moderns would head to the Top Rank ballroom opposite the train station, looking for pep pills and a fight. Oblivious to the peace-and-love revolution of the counterculture, and the arrival of the now famous Reading Festival, the local youth were still very much committed to mod clothes, ska music and chewing diet pills to get high.

I had one foot in this world. A pal named Jim worked at the local yob clothing store selling Crombie coats and Harrington jackets to neighborhood lads. I had my posse of straight friends. On Saturday nights we would wear our Sta-prest pants, Ben Shermans and Fred Perrys, and head to the "Rank," where I would chat to all the girls about how great their new missy separates looked and pray to God that nobody would figure out that I was as queer as a three-pound note.

The other foot was placed in a more daring location. While working at John Lewis, I was living a double life. Every couple of weeks, I would make an excuse, throw on my Mr. Freedom polka-dot sweater—or maybe the knockoff Mr. Freedom satin jockey jacket I had stitched myself because I was so desperate to have one but did not possess the requisite dosh—and nip off to the Railway Tavern with some of my gay John Lewis pals.

These included my lifelong best friend Biddie, aka James Biddlecombe, who worked in the John Lewis soft-furnishings department. Biddie and I took many meaningful steps together. We had both been dressing in women's clothes and staging pantomimes since we were about eight years old. Biddie looked amazing in a frock and went on to become a star of the London cabaret and panto circuit. As preteens we spent two weeks at Butlins Minehead Holiday Camp. As glam rockers we dropped acid together. Together we made our inaugural trip to the Railway Tavern where we found the local gays. There they were, still stuck in the 1950s, squeezed into fluffy sweaters and lacey stretch nylon shirts, listening to Judy Garland, knocking back gin and tonics . . . and more.

Some of the gays, as Biddie and I were fascinated to discover, were locked in the vicelike grip of a strange and noteworthy addiction. They drank endless bottles of a mysterious liquid called

Dr. J. Collis Browne's Chlorodyne. Collis Browne's was an old-school, over-the-counter "cough medicine" which had been formulated in the nineteenth century and just happened to contain a nice dollop of opium. We had read Coleridge at school and knew all about his opium addiction and the resulting constipation. The fact that these gays were ingesting vast amounts of this antique remedy seemed very Victorian and hilarious to us.

One night we spotted a superannuated gay rummaging in the trunk of his car and stared in fascination at several crates of little brown bottles, each bearing the distinctive ye olde worlde Collis Browne label. Biddie caused a screeching furor when, later the same evening, he described his amusement at this sighting to another old queen, who, as chance would have it, was an even bigger Collis Browne's guzzler than the first bloke. These homos hailed from the days when gays were discreet and wore green carnations. They were less than thrilled to have their secret addiction outed to all and sundry by some young Bowie wannabe. We quickly became personae non gratae.

It was hard to say which was the more frightening subspecies: the speeding, tweaking mods and soccer skinheads at the Top Rank or the highly strung, opiate-addicted poofters at the Railway Tavern. One thing was for sure: I would need to escape before somebody gay-bashed my head in or got me started on the Collis Browne's.

Tangential though it was, the acquaintanceship with Eric, a bona fide missy separates designer, seemed to offer me a potential escape route. I was in awe of this Eric. Eric was a working-class slag who had made it out of our crap town and who was, at least from my vantage point, hitting the big time. I use the word "slag" broadly and loosely, as we did back then. Ironically, my sister's name is Shelagh, spelled the Irish way. Everyone, including my parents, called her Slag. Even blind Aunt Phyllis called her Slag.

I yearned to follow in slag Eric's footsteps. I had stared at the distant glittering mirage of fashion, smoldering seductively on the horizon, for most of my short life (I was twenty-one), and I was yearning to reach out and touch it. Eric the missy separates designer had brought me one step closer.

At this point, dear reader, I should point out that my hometown of Reading is by no means far from the fashionably madding crowds of London. It was, in fact, only half an hour by train. But, like John Travolta's character in *Saturday Night Fever* staring across at Manhattan from his home in Bay Ridge, I felt that it might just as well be a million miles away. So near and yet so far.

Like a good working-class slag, Eric the missy separates designer made the train journey home once a week to see his mum. He never failed to swing by the luggage department to update his pal, the tall amiable queen, on his latest goings-on. He seemed to take a sadistic pleasure in taunting and tantalizing us with tales of the big city and all the glamorous people with whom he was now consorting. I was happy to be the object of his sadism. His stories gave me hope.

Eric told us about a wild and fascinating fellow designer whose name was Pamela something or other and who worked for—yes!—the Mr. Freedom label, my glam-rock obsession. In homage to the great record company founded by Berry Gordy, this gal had recently changed her name to Pamla Motown. To

me this seemed daring, wildly camp and outrageously glamorous. A white girl named Pamla Motown. How Afro-eccentric!

Another of Eric's designer pals, a guy named Cliff, had a psy-
chotic obsession with Marilyn Monroe. He had bleached his hair
blond and, if Eric was to be believed, walked around the streets
of London carrying a squirt bottle filled with peroxide. He used
it to douse the heads of hostile construction workers and random
passersby. His goal was to turn everyone he met into Marilyn,
such was his commitment to the deceased movie icon. How
Dada and recklessly outré!

Though clearly deranged, these two, Pamla and Cliff, had
accomplished something major. They had found a place to exist,
a stylish, safe, satiny, sequined space, where their insane ideas
were considered an asset. I knew in my heart that crazy Cliff and
Afro-eccentric Pamla were kindred misfits. The world of fashion had given them refuge. Soon it would be my turn.

God knows I needed a safe haven. I was just as crazy as they
were, if not more so. I was obsessed with germs and washed my
hands as often as Lady Macbeth. I was subject to overwhelming
bouts of anxiety and frequently dreamed about eating my own
hair. Looking back, I realize that I wasn't so much losing my
mind as losing my mind over the idea of losing my mind.

Mental illness being so rife in my family, I was convinced that
it was only a matter of time before I followed suit. If I did not
find an outlet for my nuttiness and my gayness, if I was forced to
live in our crap town for the rest of my days, then I would probably end up like poor batty Uncle Ken. He sat by the fire, rolling
his own cigarettes in a nasty-looking metal contraption, staring
into the middle distance and chatting to invisible entities.

I desperately needed to escape my grim town and my nutty family milieu. Fashion seemed just as nutty, but in a good way, a glam-rock way.

TWENTY YEARS LATER.

It's the early nineties. I am working at Barneys New York. I have long since exchanged my crap town for a life of fashion and fabulosity. I am not famous or ridiculously wealthy, but I am creatively fulfilled. I have found refuge in a world of rolling racks and glamour.

Though I am involved in all aspects of the Barneys store image, it is in the area of window display that I have made my name. My displays are jarring and punky and intentionally shocking: coyotes abducting babies, mannequins in coffins, fashion suicides, Christmas in July, a trailer-park tornado. My chosen themes have consistently erred toward the bizarre and unconventional. Early on in my display career I made a list of window-display taboos and then proceeded to bust them. Condoms, broken toilets, live vermin . . . it is hard for me to think of something inappropriate which I have not plonked in a display window at one time or another. Tammy Faye Bakker? I created an homage to her in the late eighties. There she was, standing next to a giant mascara wand. I have even plopped a replica of Margaret Thatcher in a black leather dominatrix frock in a holiday window. I see myself as a carny, rather than an artist, presiding over my very own Coney Island sideshow. One day I got sick of making displays that were so relentlessly pristine and simply filled the window with all manner of horrible detritus, including, but not limited to, broken furniture, cigarette butts, old newspapers, shopping coupons, soda cans and half-eaten Twinkies. The perfect backdrop for precious designer clothing.

Did I lose my marbles? Negative. Window display provided me with a therapeutic outlet for all my crap-town rage and insanity. Uncle Ken and Granny had their basket weaving. I had my windows.

So there I was, working at Barneys as Head of Creative Services, which sounds dirty but is just a fancy way of saying "marketing."

One hideously chilly winter morning an incredibly young Kate Moss entered the Barneys advertising department, wearing what looked like a monk's habit. Her perfect bone structure peeked out from an alpaca hood. On anybody else this garb would have looked costumey, almost *Canterbury Tales*. On teen Kate it looked effortlessly fab.

Accompanying Kate was Corinne Day.

Corinne was the photographer who played such a key role in launching Kate's career. She shot the now famous 1990 *The Face* magazine cover of Kate wearing an Indian headdress. The as-yet-unknown Kate was in New York to do her first shoot for Calvin Klein. Corinne, aided and abetted by Ronnie Newhouse and Glenn O'Brien, had just shot the Barneys spring catalog.

Corinne was from Ickenham in West London. Kate is from Croydon in South London. When they heard my accent, they asked me where I was from. When I told them I hailed from Reading in Berkshire, there was a flicker of recognition from both: we had all clawed our way out of our respective crap towns and into the accepting arms of mother fashion.

We chuckled about our gritty birthplaces and joyfully compared notes. Whose town was the crappiest? I insisted on mine. After all, Oscar Wilde, who was incarcerated in Reading and wrote a bleak poem about his experience, described it as "a cemetery with lights." From my childhood bedroom window I had a nice view of that very jail, thank you very much.

There is a kind of reverse chic about crap towns, which is hard to understand unless you were born in one. In biblical terms, it is the opposite of what you might call a Lot situation. Nobody looks back at a crap town and turns into a pillar of salt. Nobody denies those crap roots. There is no shame in hailing from a crap town. Au contraire! It is an immense source of pride. We escapees have enormous affection for our birthplaces. Whether we hail from Fresno or Scranton, Ickenham or Twickenham, we celebrate our gritty roots while simultaneously rejoicing in the fact that we escaped.

Crap-town pride is especially pronounced among fashion folk. The chasm between the bleak naffness of that hopeless, inhospitable, rainy birthplace and the fun and magical artificiality of the fashion world is a source of delight and inspiration. Our unpretentious origins provide a knowing reference point from which to approach the ultrapretentious white-hot furnace of fashion and trendy glamour.

The list of creative slags who have fled their crap towns and dusty villages and found safe harbor in the world of fashion is a long one:

Cristóbal Balenciaga was born in Getaria, a fishing town in the Basque province of Gipuzkoa Getaria.

Joe McKenna is from Kirkintilloch.

Ossie Clarke hailed from gritty Warrington in Cheshire.

Michael Kors is from Merrick, Long Island.

Robert Forrest hails from Carlisle on the English/Scottish border.

Mario Testino? Lima, Peru.

Azzedine Alaïa was born in Tunis.

Edward Enninful was born in Ghana.

Jean Paul Gaultier was *né* in Arcueil, Val-de-Marne. No, I've never heard of it either.

The lovely Pat McGrath was born in Northampton.

Jay McCarroll from *Project Runway* grew up in rural Pennsylvania.

Like the charismatic Jay, Kate and Corinne exude humor and confidence. They have that creative self-assurance which comes from being born on the naff side of the tracks but knowing that your innate sense of style and your outlier creativity were sufficiently major to propel you out of obscurity.

Despite their *jeunesse* and total lack of experience, Kate and Corinne had—at the time of this first encounter—just accomplished something huge. They had changed the face of fashion forever. Their collaboration created . . . another drumroll! . . . the waif.

Let's digress a moment to chat about *The Waif.*

The waif was major. The waif was the biggest thing to happen to fashion since punk. But in order to fully understand the waif, we need to digress again and explain the glamazon, the tarty virago who preceded the waif.

The glamazon came along in the late eighties. Her look could best be described as "high drag." Open any magazine back then and you were bound to encounter a cavalcade of maquillaged glamazons. The glamazon look was a postmodern mash-up of midcentury high-fashion dominatrix cuntiness. Helmut Newton and Herb Ritts and Steven Meisel all celebrated the power and stature of glamazons.

Just as with drag queens, every glamazon model's makeup and hair was designed to pastiche the styling of a midcentury model or movie star: Linda Evangelista was Jean Patchett or Dovima or Sophia Loren or Gina Lollobrigida. Christy Turlington, in Versace with a blond skyscraper beehive and more lip liner than Lady Bunny, was Barbarella or Ursula Andress. Naomi was Josephine Baker or Mahogany. Tatiana was Romy Schneider. It was a cinematic postmodern explosion of hyperfemininity.

Then Corinne and Kate created the waif, and David slayed Goliath.

The waif was the polar opposite of the glamazon. The glamazon shrieked with laughter. The waif barely smiled. The glamazon wore thick foundation. The waif didn't even wear foundation garments. The glamazon was a defiant optimist. The waif was a beautiful pessimist. The glamazon was a look-at-me supervixen. Everything was externalized. The waif represented the opposite. Everything was melancholy and internal and slightly damp. The waif was the supercool working-class slag from a crap town. Corinne and Kate had stripped away the artifice of the tired old glamazon and channeled themselves. Together they obliterated the tarty glamazon and created a whole new poetic, introspective concept of style—the perfect accom-

paniment to the grunge movement in music—which still rever-
berates today.

FIFTEEN YEARS LATER.

Kate is now a household name. She has become the most famous model in the world. She has dated Johnny Depp. She has
produced a kid with Jefferson Hack. She has extricated herself
from Pete Doherty. She has weathered various scandals and always emerged triumphant. She is still the cool girl, the chick
every gal wants to emulate.

What about me? I have reached my half century, two decades
of which have been spent working at the same store. I am, in
some ways, the Susan Lucci of Barneys. (I refer to the longevity
of my role rather than to a lack of awards. At this point I have a
shelf groaning with Lucite obelisks, cut-glass rose bowls and
brutalist granite blocks, all bearing my name.)

The last three months of my life have been consumed with
preparations for the arrival of Kate Moss and her Topshop clothing collection, which will make its U.S. debut at Barneys. The
hip and affordable UK high-street retail phenomenon is set to
conquer Manhattan with a collection designed by none other
than Kate herself. Will there be any missy separates? Undoubtedly. There will be a bit of everything. Fashion after all these
years has become an all-inclusive goulash of trends and styles
that seem to exist concurrently: bohemian, faux-hemian, sexy
secretary, *manga*, goth, dykey assassin, glamazon, and, yes, waif
are all available for your delectation.

Along with designing the Kate Moss Topshop boutique and the opening windows, I am also charged with chatting to the press.

The *New York Post* calls.

In a sincere attempt to put the sheer majesty of Topshop into some kind of broader sociological context, I tell the reporter that Kate's ineffable sense of style comes from the fact that she is "a working-class slag from a crap town, just like me."

I go on to explain that fashion would not be fashion without the contribution made by us slags. We enliven the landscape with our refreshing lack of preconceived ideas. We neutralize the corrosive bourgeois preoccupation with luxury that can so often threaten the creativity which drives real fashion. Slag power rules!

The point I was trying to make was: All the energy and creativity in fashion comes from the crap towns like Reading and Croydon. The Sebastians and Arabellas—the toffs from Knightsbridge and Mayfair—make zero cultural contribution. It's the lads and lasses who have fought their way out of the rough end of town who provide the creative foundations for La Mode. I cite John Galliano (a plumber's son) and Alexander Mc-Queen (a taxi driver's son) as good examples. Blah! Blah! Blah! I get all fired up and morph into a ranting fashion-world Camille Paglia.

The media and the blogosphere eat up my comments, or rather, I should say, a severely edited version of my comments.

The fact that my words were intended not to insult the working-class slags of the world but rather to generate a bit of crap-town solidarity was largely overlooked. Taken out of context, as they subsequently were by a billion tabloids and websites, my words sound almost menacing.

Barneys creative director disses Kate, calling her "a working-class slag from a crap town."

They forgot the "just like me" part.

The repercussions are swift and bowel-curdling: UK pals e-mail me suggesting I get my bile ducts removed. Apparently the word "slag" is no longer flung around with quite the un-p.c. abandon that it was back in my John Lewis days. Not having lived in the UK since the seventies, I am, so it would appear, working with an out-of-date lexicon.

Next an admonishing call from Topshop owner Sir Philip Green. Why-did-you-call-Kate-a-slag is the gist.

This call was followed by one similar from Kate's agent. Worse was yet to come.

My sixteen-year-old niece Tanya, a scrappy South Londoner, sent me a note declaring her love for Kate and calling me not just "a working-class slag" but also "an idiot."

Then Croydon got involved.

Croydon officials used their local paper to publicly denounce my comments as "inappropriate on many levels" and reassure the world that Croydon was "a vibrant place to live with great shopping." (This desperate attempt to rebrand their town as a red-hot tourist destination had, in my opinion, the effect of making Croydon seem, if anything, even more poignant.)

Some enterprising Brits, un-p.c. slags with great senses of humor, saw commercial opportunity in the whole debacle. They commemorated the brouhaha with a line of WORKING-CLASS SLAG T-shirts and sold them for fourteen quid each on a site called duplikate.net. The T-shirts came in a bewildering variety of colors, or "colorways," as fashion people inexplicably insist on calling them, and were accompanied by a spirited defense of yours truly.

In my own defense I would like to bring the attention of all concerned to the fact that there exists a book called *Crap Towns: The 50 Worst Places to Live in the UK,* which extensively highlights both my hometown and Kate's. According to *Crap Towns,* making eye contact in either Reading or Croydon is always a bad idea: if you make the mistake of staring at anyone in either town, "Whatchoo lookin' at, you fuckin' cunt?" will be the last thing you hear before you're poked in the eye with a half-snouted cigarette.

When Kate arrived for the opening, she was wearing a wicked little Topshop frock printed with barbed wire. Was this a portent? Hopefully not. I braced myself for a half-snouted cigarette. Instead, I am happy to report that she gave me a big hug.

Two nights later I run into Miss Moss at the Costume Institute Gala. This is fashion's most szhooshy occasion. No missy separates allowed.

The mesmerizingly beautiful Kate looks particularly un-Croydon. Having accessorized one of her own designs—a simple black chiffon number—with a bazillion dollars' worth of borrowed Graff diamonds, she was easily the coolest chick in the room.

"Love the frock," I say.

"A hundred and fifty quid," says Kate in her best South London drawl, adding, "It's part of me collection."

She and her pal Irina then dive "into the lav for a quick fag."

. . .

ABOUT EIGHTEEN MONTHS AGO.

"You don't mind sitting with the interns do you?"

The hostess of this particular fashion magazine–sponsored dinner has taken the liberty of seating me at the C table. I am not offended. In fact, I am relieved. Hanging out with the newbie slags always guarantees more fun. I am delighted at the opportunity to break bread with a fresh batch of eccentric hopefuls. They are the oddballs and misfits who have, from an early age, been mesmerized by the notion of style. These are my people. Through a combo of chutzpah and creativity they have found a way in. It's a symbiotic relationship. We brave fashion warriors bring our creative impulses and our passion for transformation. In return we get a safe space to express ourselves.

So, as instructed, I take a seat and begin to chat with the gals around me. Funny, they don't really seem like fashion daredevils at all. In fact, they seem rather conventional. I am used to new arrivals being a little rough around the edges. These interns are so well-spoken. With their carefully ironed hair and their perfectly applied maquillage, they seem much more like fashion consumers than fashion rebels.

In order to ascertain their names, I peek at their place cards. Those surnames sound hauntingly familiar. They are boldface last names, the names of movie stars and Fortune 500 mega-moguls.

"Are you by any chance related to X?" I ask one young lass who is wearing a four-thousand-dollar Alexander McQueen outfit.

"Yes. He's my dad."

"And are you the daughter of Y?" I ask another gal.

"Yes. But please don't ask me to get you an autograph."

As I survey these lucky-sperm-club members, my heart sinks.

If the kids of the famous start nabbing all the plumb creative jobs, then what about all the marginalized freaks? What about all the outsiders, the kids of the unfamous, the working-class slags from bumfuck? What are they supposed to do? Who will offer them shelter? And, most important of all, what will be the effect on fashion?

Simply put, if the idiosyncratic freaksters from the backwoods are elbowed out of the way by the kids of the famous from Knightsbridge and Brentwood, then fashion will shrivel and die.

> *Dear Fashion Industry,*
> *Beware of privileging the privileged. Keep the door open to the self-invented superfreaks from the crap towns. This is the only way to keep fashion vital and creative. Thanks awfully.*
> *Love,*
> *SD*

postscript: In 2010, the beautiful, influential and courageous Corinne Day passed away from brain cancer at the age of forty-eight, leaving a husband and two kids.

RIP, you creative genius.

the devil
and miguel
adrover

INSTEAD OF A PRINTED INVITATION, everyone receives a coffee-stained paper napkin. It is inscribed with the words MIGUEL ADROVER SPRING 2001 MEETEAST and arrives shoved inside a nondescript, Scotch-taped office envelope. Not very gleeful. Almost sinister. In retrospect, given what went down on that melancholy winter's evening, the invite could have been seen as a dreadful portent or an 'orrible omen.

The location is the old Essex Street Market on the Lower East Side. As the crowds of show attendees gather, rumors are swirling. The show is complicated. Delays are expected. Miguel is using live animals. There is no way it will start on time. Anna Wintour is alerted. Anna Wintour leaves.

It's freezing cold, and the wait proves to be interminable. Somehow I cannot bring myself to throw in the towel. After all, Miguel Adrover is fashion's new enigma. He's the bloke whose commitment to recycling is so extreme that he famously made a jacket out of Quentin Crisp's pee-stained mattress.

Quentin Crisp, author, raconteur, wearer of trailing chiffon scarves and sporter of long, dingy fingernails, was the ne plus ultra of squalid bohemia. Though he frequently referred to himself as one of the "Stately Homos of England," he spent the last years of his life in the East Village. When he croaked at the age of ninety-one, his unclaimed belongings were tossed on the street. Adrover salvaged his mattress and refashioned the fabric into a nifty striped jacket.

Chopping up frocks to make new frocks is not new. Andy Warhol did it. Martin Margiela did it. Imitation of Christ did it. But nobody had ever thought to do it with a pee-stained mattress. When Miguel's intriguingly provenanced garment was shown in 2000, it made Adrover famous. Before long he had backers and a cult following.

Fall 2001. Back to that chilly night on the Lower East Side. Finally the lights go down.

A wailing muezzin breaks the silence and jump-starts the proceedings. There is soft drumming, followed by increasingly frantic drumming. Out comes a bunch of floaty natural-linen djellabas. A Middle Eastern theme is apparent. Miguel has recently traveled to Egypt. It shows. The drumming gets louder. Slowly but surely, we are transported to the dusty backstreets of Cairo and the frenzy of the souk.

The casting is very bold. Fashion models are outnumbered by "real people." An endless stream of mysterious characters— twins, potentates, librarians, policewomen, high priestesses, mystics and concubines—are all attired in Adrover's new Middle Eastern–ish designs. As American fashion shows go, this one is very original and extremely creative. It's like watching a Pasolini movie. Soon it would morph into a Jacques Tati movie. But let's not get ahead of ourselves.

The Adrover clothing is as diverse as the casting, a something-for-everyone parade of men's tailored jackets, stained and torn kaftans, high-necked ruffled Pollyanna dresses, Foreign Legion uniforms, blousons and majestic robes made out of muddied sateen or recycled quilted packing blankets. Turbans and veils abound.

Though Miguel is a beginner, this show, with its bold, cinematic celebration of filth and grandeur, is genuinely impressive. It has gravitas . . .

. . . and then it doesn't.

Suddenly, without warning, slapstick invades the casbah.

A sturdy lady in a hijab and a nicely cut suit appears on the runway. She is not alone. Accompanying her is a large hairy black goat. There is a whiff of Edward Gorey about this sinister animal. It has horns. It has cloven feet. It has long coarse silky hair. It is the devil.

This beast may well have been more than cooperative in rehearsal. I am sure he trotted alongside his minder with nary a sideways glance. Now Mr. Devil Goat is faced with a seething souk of unknown faces, and it's a whole other story.

This animal takes one look at the crowd of fashion luminaries and slams on the brakes. This is one huge goat. The instant deceleration causes the veiled lady to stumble and screech to an inelegant halt. She glares at Satan. Satan refuses to budge.

Instant traffic jam.

The show comes to a complete standstill. Everything stops except the paparazzi. For some reason, they appear to be taking more pictures than usual. Flash! Flash! Flash!

The lady becomes very agitated. She knows that if she and her cloven companion don't start moving again, the show cannot continue. Models are already accumulating behind her like so many ketchup bottles on a factory conveyor belt. She has to act NOW.

Abandoning all pretense of fashion elegance, she turns around and, assuming a skirt-splitting tug-of-war stance, the plucky model attempts to haul the stubborn beast down the runway, à la tow truck. Tug. Tug. Resist. Resist. Flash! Flash! Flash! This standoff continues for an excruciating minute or so.

In the face of this determination, the satanic goat takes the only course open to him: suicide.

To shrieks of horror from the assembled crowd, the massive hairy black beast pitches itself, legs revolving uppermost, off the back of the runway and disappears from view.

A collective gasp removes most of the oxygen from the vast auditorium.

If it were not for her strength and her low center of gravity, Satan's date would have followed him into the abyss. This courageous lady is still standing on the runway, clutching the end of Satan's tether and staring down into the black hole at the back of the runway.

Suddenly the beast reappears, or rather its mocking head does. Plonk.

At this point in the proceedings I am reminded of the old

story of the tubby opera singer who, at the denouement of *Tosca*, flings herself, on cue, from the ramparts of the Castel Sant'Angelo only to land on the thoughtfully placed mattresses and then bounce back into full view of the audience.

The goat rests his skull on the ledge of the runway and stares at the fashion flock with a glassy gaze. It eyes the audience with a cheeky defiance, the same cheeky defiance which I have seen in the eyes of other supermodels, Linda Evangelista being a good example.

As I mentioned, Satan's companion is still clutching the leash. Her tenacity is impressive. She is clearly unwilling to admit defeat. She will not proceed without her accessory. Boldly and optimistically, she attempts to pull the animal back up onto the runway. Satan probably weighs about three hundred pounds.

Would she have been better advised to let go of the tether and keep walking, thereby allowing the show to continue? Quite possibly. But she didn't. Instead she *persevered*.

She is not the only one who is determined to force this rogue four-legged model to fulfill his obligations. An executive from Mr. Adrover's parent company, a distinguished middle-aged man in a pinstripe bespoke suit, leaps onto the runway and attempts to wrangle the beast himself.

"We booked you for this show, and you're gonna model or else!"

Flash! Flash! Flash!

The tussle continues. There is no way to describe the explosive delight of the banks of paparazzi. Never in the history of fashion has there been such an uncooperative mannequin.

Eventually, the wranglers admit defeat and the animal slides under the runway never to be seen again.

The show eventually concludes without further incident. It was beautiful and memorable, and was punctuated by one of the best comic vignettes ever to have played out on a fashion runway.

As I wandered home, I lamented the absence of Mr. Crisp, the man who unwittingly played such a key role in Mr. Adrover's success. If it had not been for Quentin and his mattress, the goat fiasco would never have taken place. I pictured the ghost of Quentin, sitting in the front row, smiling discreetly and coquettishly.

I always had a soft spot for Quent. We were connected in all kinds of strange ways. Back in seventies London, we often rode the same #22 bus to Chelsea. I would contrive to sit next to him in order to extract some piece of drollery. Despite his barbed wit, I always felt very comfortable around the stately homo. This may well have been because he bore such an uncanny resemblance to my own mother, especially when he played Elizabeth I in Tilda Swinton's breakout movie *Orlando*.

"*It's Mum!*" screeched my sister into my answering machine, after she had seen the movie. "Rush out *now* and see it! You won't believe the resemblance!"

Like his doppelgänger, Betty Doonan, Quentin was also highly quotable, a little Oscar Wilde and a little Erma Bombeck.

"Never keep up with the Joneses. Drag them down to your level."

"There was no need to do any housework at all. After four years, the dirt doesn't get any worse."

As the glamorous anarchy of the Adrover show sank in, several more Quentin-style bon mots floated back into my consciousness.

"It's no good running a pig farm badly for thirty years while saying, 'Really, I was meant to be a ballet dancer.' By then, pigs will be your style."

"Exhibitionism is like a drug. Hooked in adolescence, I was now taking doses so massive they would have killed a novice."

"Sometimes I wore a fringe so deep it obscured the way ahead. This hardly mattered. There were always others to look where I was going."

And speaking of fringe . . .

Frantic postshow inquiries revealed that the long-haired goat slept through the rest of the show, after which he was fed and then conveyed back to the farm, his fashion career in tatters.

the nude
wall phone

"SO, GET THIS. Last night I sneezed and my back popped out, so the doctor gave me a girdle. It's not funny, asshole! I'm wearing it now. Go ahead, feel it. Feel it! Don't be chickenshit. Feel my fuckin' *girdle*!"

I reached out and touched Morty. I ran my hand across the broad, rock-hard landscape of his freshly corseted torso. It felt dense and unyielding, like a bag of cement. And there were whalebones. Yes, there was no denying it. Morty was definitely wearing a girdle.

"Oh, and another fuckin' thing." Morty opened a desk drawer and took out a small filthy plastic cup with an inch of pinkish liquid in the bottom. He thrust it under my nose.

"I've got blood in my urine. *Look*."

I winced and recoiled, as one does from a forward-thrusted cup of someone else's blood-infused urine.

"So, can I go home, fer chrissakes?"

Welcome to my world.

Welcome to the glamorous world of high-fashion retail.

Morty was an ancient heterosexual window dresser and a truculent hypochondriac, a rare breed indeed. At the time, I was his boss, which was a surreal experience at best. Any attempts to give instruction or assign work to Morty were met with requests to examine recently emerged kidney stones or check out a bulging lymph node or a volcanic pustule. He was treading water until retirement. I had inherited Morty, with his girdles and neck braces and dusty cups of urine. He was grandfathered in.

Though window dressers tend to be male, our team was mostly female and often highly strung. At the top of the food chain was Monique. Though I was the official boss, Monique was definitely the éminence grise. Like a wardress in a 1950s women's-prison B movie, she clanked around with a large bunch of keys on her belt. She locked up the tool cabinet at night. She kept track of everyone's vacation days. She organized the Secret Santa. She would tip me off if one of the window dressers was thieving or copulating with another window dresser in the mannequin room when nobody was looking.

Nurturing, sarcastic and lethal if double-crossed, Monique was one tough dyke. Nothing seemed to faze her. She had worked in display for years, and she'd seen it all: the booze, the dope, the tinsel, the laughter, the glue-gun burns and the fairy-light electrocutions.

Monique loved deep-sea fishing. She spent her weekends throwing buckets of rotting chum into Long Island Sound. Angling was not Monique's only passion: she maintained a lively and academic interest in serial killers and spent her evenings

glued to the Court TV coverage of the Jeffrey Dahmer trial. A
portrait of John Wayne Gacy adorned her desk.

Monique had an assistant, a tall, regal black girl named Yana
who dealt with invoices and phone answering. (This was eons
before cell phones, and twelve of us shared a plastic nude-colored
wall-mounted instrument which dangled next to Yana's desk.)
She wore a massive pendant inscribed with a revealing message
that read I WAS BORN ENTITLED. Yana was my first exposure to
the phenomenon of the BAP, the Black American Princess. Her
goal was to marry, as soon as possible, somebody rich so that
she could hand in her notice and become a lady of leisure.
She planned to come shopping at the store every day, pausing in
front of the windows to mock her former coworkers.

Yana was extremely disturbed by the filth and the Chelsea
Hotel–ish, anything-goes ethos of our sprawling basement studio. She particularly disliked the smelly menagerie which came
to occupy some of the empty mannequin bins.

The no-pets policy which governed the rest of this particular
retail establishment meant nothing to us. Two neo-punk-rock
chicks called Sheree and Elise raised stick insects in a cracked
aquarium. A boy called Priscilla—Monique gave all the boys
girls' names—treated the display studio as a pet day-care facility
for his cocker spaniel, hamster, and an aging parakeet.

And speaking of day care . . .

Tight as I was with Monique, she scared me somewhat. We
maintained a certain distance. My closest pal was an intense
young window dresser named Cynthia, Cynders to her coworkers.

Cynders had a problematic relationship with her boyfriend.

When things were bad, she would work out her hostilities by calling a particular New Jersey gun store and conducting loud, mysterious conversations about firearms.

"I need a revolver. How quickly can I get one?" Cynders would ask the person on the other end of the line, waving a cup of coffee in her other hand.

"And some bullets. Yeah, lots of bullets," emphasized Cynders, adding in a chirpy way, "By the way, how much are bullets?"

Thankfully, Cynders never morphed into Valerie Solanas. She was just a stressed-out single mother letting off steam. Yes, Cynders had a baby boy and, unbeknownst to Human Resources, she brought him to work every day. Who looked after the little fella? While she worked her display magic in the glamorous, twinkling, aboveground emporium of elegance and style, Cynders's mother tended to the needs of her grandchild in the lunchroom of our dank basement studio. This lady was no ordinary granny: she was a full-blown, saffron-robed, chanting, finger-cymbal-chinging Hare Krishna. This is not as far-fetched as it sounds. Krishnas were quite ubiquitous back then. Where did they all go? Let's not get sidetracked.

Granny Krishna, as we called her, quickly became absorbed into our little Warhol factory of marginalized freaks. We rather liked the idea of having our very own resident mystic.

Granny Krishna sat for hours next to the microwave, rocking her grandson in an improvised saffron-*schmatta* hammock. She would chant, and *om* and *hare, hare,* and when she got bored, she played cards with Morty.

On the morning Morty showed me the urine-filled cup and

forced me to feel his girdle, neither he nor I had any idea that big changes were coming. The clock was ticking for Morty and his *malades imaginaires*—and for all of us.

LESBIANS ARE GREAT. I count many among my friends and relatives, and am sympathetic to their struggles and familiar with their strengths and weaknesses. I also have a good working knowledge of their likes and dislikes. For example, I know that they loathe sweeping generalizations about lesbians. (Any lesbian reading this paragraph will already have blown her indignation gaskets.)

In addition to their antipathy toward sweeping generalizations, lesbians also loathe patriarchal organizations and corporations. They are—not without reason—wary of being taken advantage of by "the man."

Gay men, on the other hand, rather like the idea of masculine dominance. They think big daddy is hot. Lesbians are jihadists against hetero male power. Their goal is to take down Mr. Big Stuff and they are quite prepared to slog through the fine print in order to do so. As a result, lesbians can be very nitpicky and litigious. If you work alongside a bunch of lesbians (I suggest that the collective noun for lesbians might be a "carpal tunnel" of lesbians), it is only a matter of time before a lesbian lawsuit comes through the door. They call this "taking back the night."

The lesbian willingness to read the fine print and unearth hidden inequities and injustices can be annoying, but it can also be a force for good. Such was the case with the Morty debacle.

On the morning of the girdle and the blood-infused urine,

Monique and her jangling keys came into my office and plonked a piece of paper on my desk. I winced slightly. Paperwork frightened me. My personal motto was taken from "Private Life," a popular Grace Jones song at the time: "I am very superficial. I hate anything official."

Monique hoisted herself onto the corner of my desk and gulped her cup of joe.

"This is our union contract. I took it home last night and read it."

While contract reading was like crack cocaine to Monique, the same could not be said of me.

"Oh, God. Poor you. Quel bore!"

"I am assuming that you, being the big limp-wristed pansy that you are, have never bothered to read it."

I went over to the interior window which looked out onto the studio floor and waved encouragement at my busy creative colleagues. They were a frenzy of papier-mâchéing, stapling, and glue gunning. In the near corner a window dresser was ratting an auburn B-52s wig, stabilizing it with can after can of superhold hairspray while another queen tried to attach a chicken-wire tiara onto the top.

"I am more interested in fluffing wigs and figuring out ways to make showgirl lashes out of ostrich feathers than reading contracts."

"Let me give it to you in a nutshell," said Monique, hooking her thumbs into her belt loops and puffing out her bound chest. "This contract details our pay-raise guidelines and pensions and medical. The works."

She picked up a ratting comb which happened to be on my

desk and tweaked an organic sesame seed out of her teeth using the point and then continued.

"It's a great contract, by which I mean it's a great contract if you happen to be over sixty, which none of us motherfucking are."

"Except for one person . . ."

"Morty! Morty wrote this contract."

Not only was Morty a member of my display team, but he was also, as chance would have it, the head of the window dressers' union. Yes, I kid you not, there was a *window dressers' union.* And we, the flotsam and jetsam of humanity who constituted the display department, along with the gals and gays at every other store-display studio in town, were all members of Morty's window-dressing union.

Monique proceeded to show me how the contract was only beneficial to a certain girdle wearer.

"What's to be done?"

"We need to decertify out of the union."

Suddenly I saw Monique on the ramparts, like a reverse Norma Rae. I saw placards too.

WINDOW-DRESSER FREAKS LEAVE UNION.

STAPLE-GUN QUEENS AND GLUE-GUN DYKES GO ROGUE.

HEAD WINDOW DRESSER KNEECAPPED AFTER ATTEMPTING TO DEUNIONIZE.

"Grab your clutch-purse. We have a meeting in HR in five minutes."

Monique threw all of her considerable weight behind this new cause. Over the next few days, she and I spent entire afternoons locked in meetings with union lawyers and store personnel. She banged the table a lot while I stared into the middle distance. I had no idea what they were talking about. I missed my wigs.

It was a tense time. Morty took off his girdle and replaced it with a foot cast. He walked around with a knowing smirk on his face, saying nothing, doing nothing.

Then, without any warning, he dropped a massive bomb-shell.

Morty announced that our display union was being swallowed up by the United Steelworkers. I had no idea what this meant. It sounded terrifying.

According to Morty, there was no way in hell we were going to be allowed to secede. And if we knew what was right for us, we would "not fuck with the big boys."

"But what if the big boys want to fuck with us?" joked Priscilla.

Chuckles aside, we knew there was no denying the fact that Morty had played an ace. How could Monique, just a simple dyke with psycho-killer daydreams and a fishing rod, go up against the biggest union in the history of unions?

Monique and I repaired to the Greek diner across the street to strategize.

"Morty thinks he can intimidate me with the steelworkers' union. Hah!"

"I guess we use lots of pins and staples," I posited, struggling to find some common ground between the screechingly nelly world of window display and the hairy, übermacho steelworkers.

"No disrespect, but you are an idiot," snapped Monique, adding, "and the 'fucking' part is silent."

I called home to the UK and tried to explain the whole thing to my mother. Betty Doonan had been a union shop steward in a typing pool in the sixties. When her girls were underheated or overworked, she would blow her whistle and shriek, "Everybody OUT!" Given Betty's background, I thought she might have some helpful advice. On this occasion Mrs. D. was a little stumped. She found herself torn between loyalty to her staple-gun-wielding son and her natural inclination toward union solidarity.

After listening patiently and puffing her way through a couple of Woodbine cigarettes, Betty posed a simple question. Why were we not simply renegotiating the contract? Why were we quitting the union?

The next day I cornered Monique and asked her the exact same question. Why throw out the glue gun with the bathwater?

Monique exploded with lesbian rage.

"What kind of deal do you think those chauvinist pig fuckers will give us, a bunch of freaks and trannies and part-time hookers? They will take you and your wigs and your wrist pincushion to the cleaners. We need out!"

And so we went for it.

During the complex decertification negotiations, I had to rally the troops and obtain their signatures. This was not easy. Many of my display gypsies were less than interested. When they weren't working in the store, they were in a coma in the lunchroom recovering from last night's K-hole at the Area club or the Limelight.

A Human Resources chick with a frizzed-out Joan-Cusack-in-*Working-Girl* hairdo cornered us in the elevator. She warned us to be on the lookout for any intimidation.

Monique seemed to delight in the threat of hostility, especially any hostility which might be directed toward me.

"You better watch your back! After all, you might be a window nelly, but you are also the big boss."

"But you are clearly the instigator. Why do *I* have to watch *my* back?"

"You know how these union types are. They would never hurt a lady."

"Is that what you call yourself these days?"

"Fuck you!"

"All I wanted was to make wigs and lashes. Now I'm going to end up going for a swim in the East River wearing concrete flippers."

"Don't forget your waterproof mascara."

THE DAY OF THE SHOWDOWN ARRIVED. Morty and his new union cohorts filled the display studio, and I do mean filled. They were a husky group.

The meeting was short and sweet. They took one look at us and capitulated. These burly heterosexuals were not going to spend member dues trying to keep this bunch of freaks and Krishnas in their pristine union.

Monique was triumphant.

Morty was crestfallen.

He went to the men's room and came back wearing his girdle.

The next day the steelworkers offered Morty a job at their headquarters. He looked like he had won the lottery. He tossed his girdle in the trash and was gone.

After the decertification, I was authorized by the store management to mark the occasion by taking everyone to lunch at a "gourmet" restaurant. We decided to get dressed up for the occasion. The girls began painting their eyelids. So did some of the boys. Even Monique applied a dab of lipstick.

When Yana found out the name of our fine-dining destination, she set us straight.

"Sorry to break it to you but that's not a *gourmet* restaurant," she said, taking off her hat and coat, "that's a *pseudo-gourmet* restaurant."

Rather than risk being seen at a pseudo-gourmet restaurant, Yana elected to stay behind in the basement studio and man the nude wall phone in case any urgent calls came through. I was relieved. When left alone in the studio, Granny Krishna tended to answer the phone in Sanskrit.

The outing to the pseudo-gourmet restaurant was a howling success. A great time was had by all, as evidenced by the fact that the maître d' asked us to "keep it down" no less than three times. Sheree and Elise—they were dressed like refugees from a Pat Benatar concert with shades, black jeans and tight leather jackets—got plastered and disappeared with some businessmen who were carousing at another table. Monique befriended the lady chef and flirtatiously told her that she might consider selling her the next weekend's catch for a rock-bottom price.

After lunch, I assessed the general level of inebriation and sent everyone home.

Tired, drunk, and relieved, Cynthia and I returned to the studio. As we neared the side entrance to our subterranean *salon des refusés*, a strange sight met our eyes. We found a barely recognizable Yana standing on the street. She was furious, wet and disgusted.

"My weave is ruined! Everything is destroyed."

Seated on a nearby fire hydrant, clutching a snoozing saffron-robed baby, was Cynthia's mother. She rocked back and forth, murmuring *hare, hares* under her breath.

I opened the door to the display studio and peered down the stairs. The sound of a light tropical rain was clearly audible.

"All of a sudden . . . *shshshshsshshs*!" screeched Yana, doing a convincing imitation of a furiously spraying fire sprinkler.

"What could have set off the sprinkler system?" I asked, sounding oddly sleuthlike.

"Mom, were you burning incense again?" demanded Cynthia accusingly. Granny Krishna adjusted her sari, drawing the soggy veil over her face.

By the time the sprinklers were turned off, there were three inches of water throughout the basement. It was an unmitigated disaster. Soggy boxes of display wigs bobbed about. Waterlogged mounds of paperwork, invoices and unpaid bills covered Monique's desk. Papier-mâché props were dissolving into giant mounds of pus. Holiday ornaments bobbed around like miniature buoys. By some miracle all the livestock survived.

I sloshed over to the wall phone and called Human Resources.

"You better come over here," I said, "there are mice swimming round my office."

"Oh, you guys! Always joking around!"

I hung up. There was only one thing for it. We turned off the lights and fled.

The aftermath of the flood was quite biblical. The drowned

mice decomposed in various unreachable nooks and crannies. Maggots and then flies were the unhappy result. Flood, vermin, flies, plague! It was hard not to see these biblical events as Morty's revenge.

How did we cope? We did what any typical proud American family would have done: we kept calm and carried on while wearing fluorescent hot-pink blunt-cut mannequin wigs.

thierry
mugler's flying
shoulder pads

THE MUGLER WOMAN is a wicked bitch. She stands atop the Empire State Building wearing a stainless-steel evening gown and sporting cut-glass fingernails. Her eyelashes are made of scorpion stingers. Her elaborate coiffure is fashioned from platinum wire. She doesn't care if she gets struck by lightning. She *is* lightning. Her laserlike pupils are searching the sky for passenger planes. She will destroy them with her gaze. She is Cruella de Fabulous. She is Cunty von Mugler.

Thierry Mugler—the founding designer of this storied house—took the cruelty and beauty and madness of fashion, and magnified it and pumped it full of steroids and doused it with gasoline, torched it and owned it. His vision had staggering breadth and imagination. Within Thierry's universe, there were myriad archetypes: vampires, space aliens, Sicilian widows, B-movie sluts, praying mantises, superheroines, ascending virgins, homicidal secretaries and jump-suited communistic cult members. The Mugler frame of reference was broad and rich, and the designs, perfectly expressing each theme and variation, were always exquisitely and meticulously executed.

Every aspect of the cruel, jagged, crazy Mugler vision was taken to its most bizarre and most creative and most lunatic conclusion in the notorious Mugler fashion shows.

The Mugler gals of Thierry's era—Pat Cleveland, Betty Lago, Dalma, Iman, Jerry Hall, Violetta Sanchez, Dauphine, L'Wren Scott, Naomi—smoldered down the runway looking as if they had just eaten their own young. In amongst the models du jour, Thierry thrust his favorite style icons—Tippi Hedren, Julie Newmar, Diana Ross, Patricia Hearst, Ivana and Ivanka Trump being a random sampling thereof.

And the music!

The typical Mugler fashion-show soundtrack featured an improbable mash-up of Puccini, Uum Kulthum, Carmen Miranda and Yma Sumac.

Who was Yma Sumac?

Yma Sumac was a Peruvian proponent of exotica. In the 1950s she took her four-octave range and used it to churn out fabulously atmospheric albums with titles like *Voice of the Xtabay* and *Legend of the Sun Virgin*. Alongside the tropical stylings of Martin Denny, Don Ho and Les Baxter, Yma's music was heard at tiki bars across America during the fifties and sixties.

Yma, as depicted on the covers of her albums, was every inch the Mugler woman. Bitchy, remote and with an expression which says, "Don't fuck with me. I like to ride on the back of a giant condor just for kicks and, besides, I am too busy enjoying my own private sick and twisted fantasy world to bother with the likes of you."

I am an Yma fan of long standing. Her birdcall screechings, basso profondo growlings and incomprehensible Andean yodeling formed the backdrop to my life after I found a cache of her albums in a jumble sale in the early seventies.

In the eighties I was flicking through *The Village Voice* when—gasp, yodel, birdcall, screech!—I saw that Yma Sumac, she herself, would be appearing at a venue called the Ballroom.

I called Thierry in Paris and alerted him to the fact. He boarded the next plane.

Thierry decided that for his next show he would build a giant replica of Popocatépetl. At the finale, the volcano would erupt and Yma would emerge, singing all the while. Would she be open to such an idea? He had come to New York to find out.

Thierry combined his trip with a shoot or two. An accomplished photographer—Thierry often shot his own ads—he strapped a couple of girls to the top of the Chrysler Building, where they struck heroic attitudes while wearing scalpel-cut Mugler suits, dangling thousands of feet up in the air.

Thierry always loved to put a gal on the top of a building. This was less about suggesting an imminent suicide and more about deifying the model in question. His dream had always been to shoot a chick in Mugler couture atop the Mormon Temple in West Los Angeles, a singularly Mugler-esque piece of architecture. Permission has so far not been granted. One day.

The big night arrived. Yma's New York comeback!

We—me and a whole gang of Yma fans including Joey Arias,

Alix Malka, Chiclet Johanknecht, Nell Campbell, Lypsinka, David LaChappelle, Larissa, David Yarritu, Susanne Bartsch and John Badum—all ensconced ourselves excitedly in the cozy Ballroom auditorium. Expectations were running high. The Styrofoam pre-Colombian effigies flanking the stage only served to ratchet up our feverish anticipation.

Eventually the lights dimmed, the jungle drums started, and Yma appeared.

Enrobed in exotic chiffons, she looked exactly like her album covers, only slightly fleshier. Her demeanor was haughty and cold. Her eyeliner and lashes were showgirl perfect.

Thierry noted with satisfaction that she was wearing a midriff-exposing top. If she was bold and ballsy enough to reveal this much of herself at her age—she was born in 1922, so the Yma we were watching would have been in her mid-sixties—maybe she would be intrepid enough to allow Thierry to launch her heavenward from the bowels of an erupting volcano like so much diva lava.

The drumbeats continued. Yma struck angry princess poses, which reminded me of Maria Montez in *Cobra Woman*. We waited anxiously for her to sing.

Would she still be able to hit that dog-whistle top note? Could she still growl like an Amazonian leopard?

Bam!

Without any it's-great-to-be-here preamble or warm-up banter, she launched straight into an aggressive rendition of "Goomba Boomba" from the album *Mambo!* Soaring and hooting and shrieking, she knocked it out of the park and straight up the Amazon.

We, of course, gave her a standing ovation. Did Yma care? Not really.

Despite the fawning, foaming fan worship frothing from the front row, Yma remained remote and rather bored looking. However, her queenly bearing only served to fuel our ardor.

Next came "Taita Inty," from *Voice of the Ixtabay*. As fans of the song will know only too well, "Taita Inty" has a slow build, like Ravel's "Bolero." By the time she reached the crescendo, arms akimbo like a wicked chiffon-clad insect, we were on our feet again.

Next came "Jivaro," a personal favorite of mine. When she reached the growl—*grrrr* J-I-V-A-R-O *grrr*—we let out a collective cheer. This did not go over well.

Yma looked startled. She stopped singing. When she realized that our exuberance was a response to her growling with such proficiency, she looked almost annoyed.

"Doesn't everyone growl?" her pissed-off expression seemed to say.

As the set continued, it became abundantly clear that Yma was prone to mood swings. Her pianist seemed to be the focus of much of her irritation. On several occasions she would stop midsong and admonish him in some ancient Peruvian dialect, even though he was clearly a local dude. These castigations were often followed by her counting time with her finger, as if teaching the rudiments of music to a child.

Yma continued with her classic hits. Joy beamed from every face in the audience. The only person not enjoying the proceedings was Yma herself. Toward the end of her set, she suddenly developed an irrational aversion to her Styrofoam totems. Every time she caught sight of them she would recoil. This made no sense. I wanted to shout out, "What are you scared of, you crazy old Peruvian princess? After all, those are *your* ancient Styrofoam totems."

Yma's focus eventually shifted from her pianist and her totems to her dragon-lady fingernails. Between songs, and increasingly during songs, she began pressing each bloodred talon to make sure it was firmly attached. When she emerged from these distracting manicure sessions, she would glare at the pianist and make him start over. Her imperious gaze defied contradiction. It said, "You are the one who lost his place. Don't blame me and my dragon-lady Lee Press-on nails."

After the performance, Thierry went backstage to meet his idol and pop the question. Would she be willing to fly to Paris and explode from a flaming faux volcano?

We were on tenterhooks.

Thierry undertook this task alone: our collective enthusiasm had already unsteadied the great diva. If we all crammed into her dressing room and began gushing, she would probably spread her chiffon condor wings and fly straight back to Machu Picchu.

Eventually Thierry returned from his mission. We clustered round to see if Yma was up for it.

"Ymassuming she said yes."

"Ymassuming she wants a ton of cash."

"Ymassuming we are all off to Paree."

Thierry described his surreal encounter with the Voice of the Xtabay. When he introduced himself, Yma was quick, almost insultingly quick, to respond that she had never heard the name Thierry Mugler.

Thierry tried appealing to her vanity. He thumbnailed the costume he would make for her. Referring to herself in the third person, as she did throughout the interview, she rejected the frock and the offer.

"But Yma already has so many beautiful gowns . . ."

We all repaired to the Odeon to lick our wounds and relive the undeniable magic of the evening.

During dinner, I sought to assuage Thierry's disappointment by telling him that, allegedly, Yma was not from Peru at all, and that her whole schtick was the invention of a record company, fabricated to meet the public's taste for exotica.

"Some people say she was born in Brooklyn," I explained, "and that her real name is Amy Camus, and that she had flipped it. Like Isaacs to Scaasi! Maybe it's true. Maybe the whole Peruvian Inca bit is just made up."

Thierry swallowed his filet mignon and then let out an anguished sigh. "But don't you see? That makes her even *more* fabulous!"

the
unkindness
of chic

I ONCE INTERVIEWED the legendary fashion designer Sir Hardy Amies for *Nest* magazine. Not long after our cozy chat, Sir Hardy kicked the bucket. He was ninety-four years old. Did I kill him?

As I look back on the brief time we spent together, I am aware of a vague lingering sense of responsibility regarding his death. This results from the fact that, during the course of our conversation, I caused him to become somewhat agitated. I sincerely hope I did not hasten his demise in any way. Murdering a knight is a horrid thing to do.

Full disclosure: Hardy Amies is not my only maybe-I-had-a-hand-in-it celebrity death. I also suspect that I might have played a role in the snuffing out of Mr. Show Business himself, the late, great Liberace.

It all happened at one of his final concerts at Radio City. I was excited, turned on, if you will, by the unbridled richesse of his costumes. (Liberace floated on stage wearing a bejeweled purple ostrich cape.) During the curtain calls, I lost all inhibition and bum-rushed the stage with a lady friend named Henny Garfunkel. Henny has multiple ear piercings and a brazenly overpainted lip line. She bore no resemblance to the other female blue-hairs who were crushing toward their idol. She looked more like a bohemian kitchen witch.

There is no question that we—me with my rabid enthusiasm and my pal with her unconventional appearance—startled the gorgeously sequined old pianist. When confronted with our fan-worshipping ardor, Liberace drew back and his eyes popped wide open. Clearly he was freaked. His visage assumed a startled look as if he were experiencing a white-hot rectal shooting pain. A few weeks later, he too was pushing up the daisies. Did we kill him? I hope not. RIP, Lib.

Back to Sir Hardy.

Before I describe what transpired between us, permit me to give you a little background on Sir H. This accomplished and caustic-tongued fashion designer is best known for two things: First, he created the futuristic costumes for Stanley Kubrick's *2001: A Space Odyssey.* Second, and more important, he is the bloke who is credited . . . drumroll . . . with having conjured . . . trumpets, confetti cannons . . . Queen Elizabeth's iconic look.

"What 'look'? Does the queen even have a 'look'?" I hear you ask, with gasping incredulity.

"Of course she does!" I respond, with equally gasping incredulity.

Think about those boldly hued, dyed-to-match outfits; think about a bright pink dress, bright pink coat and bright pink hat, worn with those comfy beige John Lobb strolling heels. And that white purse. Voilà! Her look!

And then there is the signature cut, the bust darts, the knee-grazing skirts. These too were envisioned by Sir Hardy and over time became synonymous with Brenda. (We Brits often refer to our queen as "Brenda." Similarly, Madonna was redubbed Madge. It's about replacing the pompous with the quotidian.) That unprovocative frumpy Amies fit is as timelessly and unmistakably associated with Brenda as are her corgis. This is her time-to-meet-the-plebs look and the queen has rocked it consistently throughout her spectacular reign. This is the ensemble she wears while shaking hands and asking, "And what do you do?" or "Have you come far?"

Yes, some of her frocks were designed by other dudes, like the brilliant Sir Norman Hartnell. But Sir Hardy is the bloke who created the look which set the tone. These were the outfits which, to quote Sir Hardy, were "immortalized on a thousand biscuit tins."

The first time I saw the queen all Hardy'd up in person was back in the early sixties on a wind-lashed pier on Belfast Lough. We were enjoying our annual sojourn with toothless Grandpa. QE2 emerged from her Rolls wearing a matching blazing yellow silk coat, dress and hat. The sun popped out from behind a cloud and hit Queen Brenda. She lit up like a gorgeous blazing shantung canary.

This particular appearance took place before the sectarian violence re-erupted, so nobody was too worried about bombs. We peasants were waving and smiling, and smiling and waving, and squinting at the yellow birdie in the distance. Yes, the queen was miles away and could not see us. But it did not matter, because *we* could see *her*. And we knew it was her. In her chrome yellow dyed-to-match Hardy Amies ensemble, she was unmistakably, irrefutably THE QUEEN.

In the intervening years, Brenda has really stuck to her sartorial guns. Nobody could ever accuse the queen of being a trend surfer. She looks the same today as she did half a century ago. In the current age of global fashion and red-carpet masturbation, it is commendable that HM has clung to her iconic frowzyship with such amazing tenacity.

No duodenum-mangling Azzedine Alaïa frocks for Brenda.

No sexy skorts or camel-toe-inducing gauchos.

No Mary Kantrantzou prints or Chanel boucles.

No Westwood Buffalo Girls or basque corsets or see-through Cavalli leopard-print djellabas.

No Gareth Pugh gothic glamour shrouds or Rick Owens leather shrugs.

Betty Windsor has always remained deliriously and amazingly trend immune. She has managed to sail through beat, mod, hippie, glam rock, punk, new romantic, grunge, neohippie and twenty-first-century historical hipster with an unwavering, oblivious gaze. Long live Brenda! Long may she frowze!

I was determined to take advantage of my time with Sir Hardy and draw him out on the subject of Brenda's look. I wanted to understand the origin and motivation behind its creation. Toward the end of our conversation, I took a deep breath and asked the corgi-in-the-room question: Had he ever, in all his years of dressing Brenda, been tempted to shake things up a bit and squeeze the reigning monarch into something a little more, shall we say . . . stylish? His reaction was extreme. It was as if I had pulled out a sawed-off shotgun or snapped the pin from a grenade with my teeth and popped it into the pocket of his cashmere bought-it-in-the-Burlington-Arcade cardigan.

Sir Hardy blanched.

His brow suddenly furrowed.

He rolled his eyes, inhaled deeply and exhaled with regal irritation.

After a few nerve-racking seconds, he spoke.

"Young man! You seem not to understand."

Suddenly I was Alice. Clearly I had offended the knight and he was about to turn into the Red Queen and demand my decapitation.

Sir Hardy's nostrils flared. My buttcrack became moist.

"Know this: To design clothes for the queen of England is to be charged with a momentous and complex task."

Would I be forced to play croquet with a flamingo and some hedgehogs?

"The chief requirement is that Her Majesty must always appear *friendly and approachable*. She can never appear to be . . . *unkind*."

I nodded vigorously in agreement. He continued.

"And, as a result, Her Majesty must never appear to be *chic*."

Now it was my turn to blanch.

"Why ever not?" I asked.

"If Her Majesty appeared in public looking chic, it would be disastrous. Why? Because there is . . . a terrible *unkindness* to chic, that's why."

The unkindness of chic!

Quel shock!

I was paralyzed with fascination. Was it possible that chic-ness and kindness were mutually exclusive? Surely not.

Suddenly my chic-obsessed brain began frantically ransack-ing its files, searching desperately for iconic visuals where chic-ness and kindness were somehow combined.

Mother Teresa was kind, but was she chic? Maybe in a drapey Japanese avant-garde kind of way, but not in the Chanel/Babe Paley/Anna Wintour sense of the word.

Angelina Jolie is kind to starving people, but she never dresses in a chic way when she visits them. Au contraire! When Angie is on assignment, her clothing is never chic. It's more les-bian gritty.

Princess Diana was kind to children and sick people, but was she really ever chic? Though attractive, she was hardly the apex of arresting style. She was no Duchess of Windsor . . . thank God! Yes! I am referring to that überchic cold bitch, Wallis Simpson.

Mrs. Simpson, the woman who once said, "You can never be too rich or too thin," the self-indulgent, couture-devouring dandy who stole the heart of the man who would be king and then caused his abdication. She was the most loathed woman in England, but she was also, undeniably, the most stylish. What better example of the unkindness of chic.

One can imagine Brenda directly addressing the Simpson issue with Sir Hardy: "If I look as chic as old Nazi-lovin' Wallis, my subjects will tear me to bits. So step on it, you old poof, and let's get frumpy!"

Wallis Simpson's commitment to style trumped everything in

her life. Yes, she was chic, but she was also brittle and creepy and strange. You can imagine her doing weird things behind closed doors, like spanking her husband with a car aerial or bleaching her teeth with sulfuric acid. Surely there must be somebody who was as stylish as Mrs. S. but who was also able to crack a smile, show a bit of empathy and humanity, and feed the birds, two pence a bag, two pence, two pence, two pence an Hermès bag.

As I scoured my mental Pinterest fashion-inspiration board for imagery which combined both kindness and chicness, I repeatedly came up empty-handed. From Irving Penn to Meisel, from von Unwerth to Herb Ritts, all I could find were chic-but-icy biatches. Gazing at these iconic photographs, I began to wonder what was going through the heads of these laser-eyed harpies. What, exactly, is the inner dialogue of an unkind, über-chic woman?

When Jacqueline de Ribes, as photographed by Richard Avedon, was gazing into that mirror, flanked by her two kids, was she tenderly imagining their future or was she praying that they would piss off to boarding school and leave her to get on with her maquillage?

Was Avedon's Dovima affectionately petting the elephants? Or was she coldly, heartlessly using them as a backdrop? Would she ever willingly muck out their stinky pens or administer a pachyderm suppository? Probably not.

The ability to project malevolence is, so it would appear, more critical to a successful chic career in fashion than the ability to care for large animals or to smile benevolently. This is especially true regarding fashion models.

There is no question that the most compelling and mesmerizing mannequins have always adopted a hostile and unkind look. From Jean Shrimpton to Veruschka, from Penelope Tree to Peggy Moffitt, from Iman to Coco Rocha, the thing that unites all models through the ages is an ability to adopt a cold fuck-you expression as soon as the camera starts clicking. When Linda Evangelista stares down the camera in the movie *Unzipped*, she appears wicked enough to melt your Stella McCartney vegan-vinyl stilettos. When Kate if-looks-could-kill Moss returns your gaze from a Rimmel ad, you know she's not planning on baking you some scones or knitting you a tea cozy anytime soon. All the most successful gals—Karen Elson, Kloss, Kurková, Arizona—have the ability to reconfigure their features into a mob wife expression that says, "I will come at you and I will cut you." In this regard, the queen of England is the opposite of a successful model. She is not allowed to come at people and cut them. She must always be kind to them.

In conclusion:

To appear chic and be perceived as chic, it is necessary to adopt the mien of a remote, cold bitch. Hauteur is your mot du jour. Disdain is your main accessory. Snottiness is your life-blood.

But what happens when you spend much of your waking life sucking in your cheeks and attempting to project bitchiness? Will you inevitably morph into a twisted homicidal witch? Will your chicness eventually devour any kindness or humanity which is lurking in your persona?

Please try not to let it. Stay wicked on the outside and cosy on the inside.

Sir Hardy was right. There is an unkindness to chic, and

chicness has no place in Buckingham Palace. A chic monarch would soon find herself jiggling toward the guillotine in a very unchic grotty little tumbrel, and so will you if I catch you behaving like a bitch. So by all means dress yourself up like a wickedly chic glamour witch. Just don't become one.

Thanks awfully.

america's next top shaman

FASHION MODELS MAKE lots of money, but they are legendarily cheap. Despite being the highest-paid person in the room, the groovy model is the last one to stick her hand in her pocket. If I saw a tall, thin, attractive gal offering to pick up the tab or pay her way, I would think, *Oh, I thought she was a model. But she cannot possibly be. Look, she's parting with money. I wonder what she does for a living.*

On the rare occasions when a model rummages for her wallet, it is invariably "missing."

"OMG! I cannot believe I left my purse at home!"

I can believe it, and so can everyone else. If all your food is paid for—a river of absurdly bountiful catering is the norm on all fashion shoots—and if everyone showers you with drinks whenever you go clubbing, and some dude or other inevitably offers you a cab share, then why would you need your wallet? You *are* Holly Golightly.

All of which begs the question, If models don't spend money

on day-to-day stuff, then where the hell is it? What on earth are they doing with all that "hard-earned" dosh?

The answer to this question is quite simple. The average model saves up all her model fees until she falls in love with an underpaid photo assistant who is addicted to smack. Then, mysteriously, seamlessly, drip, drip, drip, all her shekels vanish.

Lots of models are young and stupid; actually, all of them are. This should not come as much of a surprise. I was young and stupid when I was seventeen, and I'm sure you were too. But I had one huge advantage over models: I had NO money, so nobody was going to bilk me to support a drug habit. And, more important, nobody—and I really do mean nobody—was ever listening to or taking note of anything I was saying.

With models, this is absolutely *not* the case. It is, in fact, totally the opposite. If a model opens her trap, the entire room leans in to hear what she's going to say. For some reason we hang on her every word as if she were the Oracle of motherfucking Delphi. Foolishly, we persuade ourselves that the exceptional physical exterior must surely contain an equally remarkable interior.

Every now and then, when we are trying to wrap our heads around some morsel of model-speak, we need to stop and remind ourselves how simple they are. How simple?

Once, on a Barneys shoot, the hairdresser and I were blathering on about Marie Antoinette. While we chatted, he was futzing with the model's hair, augmenting it with wigs in an effort to achieve the *grandeur de coiffure* of the legendary French queen. Marie Antoinette this. Marie Antoinette that.

The model was sitting in the makeup chair patiently listening, her eyes ping-ponging back and forth between my colleague and me. Finally she spoke.

"Is she new? Which agency is she with?"

Is it fair to generalize so brutally about fashion models?

Is it fair to mock their lack of brain power?

Of course it's not fair, but who said life was going to be fair or even remotely fact based. Isn't it more fun to exaggerate? We all know that some models are cute and kind and caring but, you have to admit, my sweeping generalizations are always so much more exciting than facts. And don't they always contain a kernel or two of truth? And, furthermore, if models get the odd bit of stick from the likes of me, don't they simply need to toughen up and learn to handle it? After all, God gave them the gift of beauty, and they never have to pay for anything. What more do they want? They should be able to stand a little light mockery.

As I mentioned above, I too was annoying and stupid when I was young. But after a while, I got smarter. This is not the case with fashion models. They become *increasingly* mentally turgid and two-dimensional as they get older. And the same would happen to you if you spent your entire life being treated differently, preferentially, because of the way you looked. Average-looking people, squat people, homely people are always much smarter, more competent and more fun than fashion models. Average people have to *make more of an effort*.

But, when all is said and maquillaged, fashion models are undeniably pleasing to look at. *This* is their saving grace.

If you go to a restaurant and there's a major model "eating" her dinner, you will always find yourself staring at her. The entire joint is surreptitiously craning. There is a force field around every model. We are all pulled inexorably into the vortex of their beauty. We worship them. I worship them.

G. K. Chesterton once said, "When people stop believing in God, they don't believe in nothing. They believe in anything."

I would respectfully like to amend this: When people stop believing in God, they don't believe in nothing. They believe in models.

Kate, Naomi, Kloss, Evangelista, Raquel, Lara . . . these are our deities.

And while we are busy believing in models, what are models believing in?

Let me paraphrase G. K. once more: When models stop believing in God, they don't believe in nothing. They believe in all kinds of crazy woo-woo shit.

The most "spiritual" people are always those with the most superficial occupations. Isn't it always the makeup artists, stylists and fashion designers who are training to become shamans or *ohm*ing and naval gazing at ashrams? Fashion models in particular are HUGE suckers for New Age idiocies. They believe in chakras and auras and any old gobbledygook which they glean from the bulletin board of their yoga studio or health-food store. A model would never leave the house without casting the runes. She would never sign a big contract without consulting her guru. If you ever have a stash of dream catchers you need to flog, just go backstage at a fashion show. You will be able to unload the entire bunch.

And if you need to get in touch with any dead relatives, just book a fashion model. Yes, fashion models are profoundly psychic. Hold that thought.

My husband and I live in a spooky old building in Greenwich Village. Some refer to it as the Downtown Dakota, in reference to the sinister-but-fabulous apartment building on the Upper West Side where Polanski shot *Rosemary's Baby* and where some monstrous person unforgivably shot John Lennon.

For many years our next-door neighbor at the Downtown Dakota was a reclusive and ancient and lovely old broad with a delightful smile who had moved into the building before the Second World War.

One day she announced that she was relocating to an old folks' home in upstate New York. Anxious to grab more square footage, my Jonny and I snapped up her pad.

I will never forget the first time we peeked inside. The interior was dark and dusty and musty. The walls were lined with ancient peeling paper. It was creepily beautiful in a Deborah Turbeville kind of way. As we walked through the deserted high-ceilinged apartment, small chunks of paint and plaster descended like snow. Looking at the melancholy, forgotten rooms, I was reminded of those old Victorian snaps of clairvoyants and ghosts and ectoplasm. I was reminded of Helena Blavatsky.

Which agency is she with?

Permit me to clarify for my model readers.

Blavatsky was a superfreak. Fantasist, fabulist, spiritualist, theosophist and all-round bullshit artist, Russian-born Madame Blavatsky had the creepy ability to pull crazy stunts like levitate tables, produce rapping noises in remote parts of her house, cause pianos to tinkle in empty rooms and summon the wind to blow out oil lamps. Always useful.

In 1873 she packed up her bag of tricks and sailed to New

York City, where she basically invented the whole notion of contemporary "spirituality" and became the superstar clairvoyant du jour.

No model she. Madame B. was a chunky Slavic version of Whoopi Goldberg's character in the movie *Ghost*. Looks notwithstanding, she tapped into the Victorian obsession with death and all things ghostly and made a bang-up career for herself. Attendees to Madame Blavatsky's séances and soirees were treated to the sight of a taxidermied baboon lurking in the entryway clutching a copy of Darwin's *On the Origin of Species*.

La Blavatsky made a living scaring the crap out of people by pretending to bring their relatives back from the dead. She was a carny and a faker, who also popularized ideas about karma and positive thinking and—hello!—the model favorite: yoga!

So, yes. I was reminded of Blavatsky. What would she have made of this macabre abode? It's hard to imagine that she would not have unearthed a few lingering souls, or at least pretended to.

Back to me and my Jonny.

The former tenant moved out, but we did not move in. Something mysterious and intangible was holding us back. Money. The place remained empty while me and my Jonny attempted to scrape together the requisite renovation shekels.

In the meantime, I had the brilliant idea of using it as a fashion shoot location. Budgets at Barneys were tight—we were in bankruptcy at the time—so why not shoot our seasonal fashion catalog in a no-cost, uniquely atmospheric location?

The day of the shooting arrived. I brushed my teeth and ran next door to see how things were progressing. The photographer was setting up his lights. Our model was sequestered in the upstairs powder room. I was anxious to introduce myself and hear anything oracular she had to say, or see if I could get her to buy me a cup of coffee, or just stare at her and admire her cheekbones.

I creaked up the rotting stairs and opened the door. Seated on the (closed) toilet and smoking a fag was a hard-faced Russian beauty. Let's call her Svetlana.

Svet wore an anxious expression. Her eyes darted about as only a model's eyes can. She spoke.

"Wha's dis place?"

"It's actually an empty apart—"

"Is haunted. Haunted bad. Very bad!"

"Well, we think with a little paint and—"

"Tell me! Somebody die here recently? Yes?"

"There was an old lady living here who—"

"I know it! I feel energy. Is violent death? Yes?"

"She is in a retire—"

"You hear her screams at night?"

"Actually she was a lovely per—"

"You need priest. I get you Russian Orthodox. The best."

"We were rather hoping to move in next spr—"

"Don't do it! If you sleep here, you wake up next morning a raving maniac with the snow white hair."

"Okay. Well, I think we're ready for the first shot."

Over the next few days, Svetlana's conviction that the previous tenant had died a horrible, unspecified, supernatural death only grew. Nothing I could do would get her to reconsider her position. Svet knew without a shadow of a doubt that our former neighbor had been raped and pillaged and obliterated by demons and that the whole place was now haunted. Exorcism was the only answer.

She lost no time in making everyone on the shoot aware that "an old lady, she perishing horrible, right HERE!" The fact that the lady in question was now happily ensconced in an old people's home, enjoying a nice ambrosia salad every night, seemed of no interest to Svet. It was hard to escape the notion that she was channeling her fellow countrywoman Madame Blavatsky.

The shoot continued. Svetlana looked hauntingly lovely juxtaposed against the faded fusty grandeur of our apartment. Her spiritual anxieties lent a certain Edgar Allan Poe—like gravitas to her facial expressions and poses. The atmosphere during the shoot was quite funereal—in a good way.

Svetlana's doom-laden rantings were infectious. When they arrived each day, the crew seemed surprised to find me still in the land of the living. Between shots, there was much crucifix fondling and hushed, respectful talk. You don't raise your voice in what is essentially a killing field.

On the last day of the shoot, I stood on the threshold of what would soon be transformed into a groovy, swinging, happy, insanely colorful, Jonathan Adler—decorated home and bid farewell to the crew.

Svetlana looked at me with a sympathetic, heartfelt gaze. We embraced. She grabbed me and slammed her heavily rouged mouth up against my ear.

"Promise me you don't move in till you SAGE THE SHIT OUT OF THIS PLACE!"

When a model tells you to do something, you just do it.

anna's wondering why we haven't started yet

LAST NIGHT I DREAMED I went to Anna Wintour again.

This is not so unusual. Like every other sick, twisted, neurotic, highly strung fashion person on earth, I regularly have Anna dreams. The bobbed and dark-spectacled *Vogue* editrix in chief haunts our collective unconscious on a near-nightly basis. Even as I write, some slumbering style slave somewhere in the world is tossing and turning, and mumbling, "Yes, Anna! No, Anna. Three Birkin bags full, Anna."

Why is Ms. Wintour so enmeshed in our collective psyche? Why is she inhabiting our nocturnal dramas and deliriums? The reason is fairly obvious, non?

La Wintour is all-pervasive and all-powerful. She represents many mythological archetypes, so many, in fact, that it's hard to keep track of them all: She is mother, soothsayer, monarch, deity, avatar, savior, teacher, redeemer, judge, kingmaker and executioner all rolled into one. So complex and powerful is her image that it is nothing short of a miracle that we ever dream about anyone else. How on earth do we ever find the psychic space to squeeze in a Gaga or a Madonna dream, to mention nothing of a Maya Angelou or a Margaret Thatcher one?

My Anna dreams are nothing if not consistent. Though the narratives and context may vary, the essential emotion is always the same: good old-fashioned shame. In my Anna dream I am invariably overwhelmed by the feeling that I have done something unforgivably unsavory and horrid.

Once, I was flitting through a crowded shopping mall wearing only a cropped Ed Hardy T-shirt. Yes, I was *sans panties*. Just at the moment of maximum public humiliation, Anna walked out of the nearest Chanel boutique looking flawlessly intimidating in shades and bouclé.

I woke up cringing. This feeling subsided only after I realized that I was, at least, wearing panties.

Cringing? Yes, we cringe and bow down before Anna because this is what you do in front of your queen. You worship and you curtsey, but you also cringe.

I am the same age as Anna. As baby boomers, we have a significant dollop of life experience under our belts. No longer in the first flush of youth, we are enriched by the machinations and tribulations of more than half a century. We have seen all kinds of things, both jarring and fabulous. We remember Kenneth Tynan saying the first "fuck" ever on live TV. We remember Christine Keeler and Mandy Rice-Davies. We remember the Manson Girls, and Betty Ford's drinking problem. We remember when heiress Patty Hearst got kidnapped, became Tania the revolutionary and started calling everyone "fascist insects."

We remember when David Bowie had a boy child and named him Zowie. We remember the Hillside Strangler. We remember Golda Meir. We remember when Alan Carr produced the Academy Awards with a Disney theme and all the pompous Hollywood actors got up and walked out because they felt it was so cheesy. We roamed the earth when women wore go-go boots and panty girdles and nylons. And we remember when men wore Hai Karate and had thick, butch tufts of hair on their various private areas. Some women too.

In other words, we have both been around the block.

Despite the shared history, Anna is different from moi and the others of our ge-ge-generation. (A reference to "My Generation," a song by the Who circa 1965. I personally prefer early Who to late Who. "Substitute" might just be the tightest pop song in history. Just saying.) Simply put, we are sheep and Anna is the sheep dog. Over the years we fashionistas *d'un certain âge* have watched in awe as Anna stepped out front and became the leader of the pack, *vrrrm vrrm!* (Another song: "Leader of the Pack" by the Shangri-las circa 1964.)

While the rest of us stumbled and bungled through our various fashion careers, enjoying successes and failures, Anna grabbed the chariot reins of her fashion editorship and drove a steady ascending course toward deification. 'Ere long, we became less than the dust 'neath her chariot wheels. (Yes, another song reference. This time it's a freaky Edwardian love lyric by Adela Florence Nicolson circa 1916: "Less than the dust beneath thy chariot wheel, less than the weed which grows beside thy door.")

Referring to Anna as a fashion editor is, therefore, a bit

like calling the queen of England a civil servant. She is major. She is not only the most famous *Vogue* editor of all time, but she is also the ultimate figurehead of American fashion, nay, universal fashion.

During the last thirty years—Anna's reign—fashion has exploded from minority elitism to international democratic spectator sport. Fashion is now a global cultural obsession. When Anna first came to New York, there were about twenty shows during any given Fashion Week. Now there are literally hundreds.

While I personally find it extremely hard to keep up, Anna, the fashion superdeity, seems to have no problem doing so. In fact, she not only keeps pace, she makes the pace. She has simultaneously weathered and orchestrated this massive period of change, enduring all that explosive growth while also helping to create it. If fashion is a worldwide smorgasbord, then Anna has played a significant role in making it thus.

She is mega. And just when you think she cannot get any more mega, she knocks it out of the park with some new level of accomplishment in fashion megastardom. Anna Wintour is an amazingly impressive broad. And that, dear reader, is why we cringe and curtsey. (Since I am no longer in the first flush of youth, my knees tend to make cracking sounds whenever I curtsey. I am toying with the notion of applying to Anna's office for a no-curtsey-necessary dispensation.)

Having opened up my psyche—thereby hopefully shedding some light on fashion's obsession with Anna Wintour—I now want to take a different perspective. Instead of holding up a mirror, let's grab a telescope. Let's try for a moment to get inside her head and to ask the question, "What's it like to *be* Anna Wintour?"

How does it feel to have created this iconic role and now be obliged to inhabit it, to service it and to maintain it?

What's it like to sally forth every day into this inferno of high expectations, expectations which you yourself have helped create?

What's it like to listen to the cracking knee joints that accompany my curtseys? What's it like to climb onto your throne every day, grab your scepter and orb, and look into the eyes of your subjects knowing that many of them, if not all, will have dreamed about you the night before?

If there are moments when AW wants to scream, "Oh, fuck it! I'm retiring to the Cotswolds to grow peonies!" you would never know it. If she has ever snapped her pearls, tossed her Chanel pocketbook down the lav, run home from the office and assumed the fetal position, then I am not aware of it.

She is unwavering in her leadership.

She is utterly consistent.

In addition to being consistent, Anna is also wildly magnanimous. I refer specifically to the fact that, back in 2006, she graciously showed up at the premiere of *The Devil Wears Prada* and did not punch Lauren Weisberger's lights out, an action she might well be capable of, given how much tennis she plays.

Ms. Weisberger, for those of you who have been in a coma for the last ten years, was Ms. Wintour's Eve Harrington: a toadying supplicant who successfully parlayed her former job as an assistant at *Vogue*, and its supposed mistreatments, into a putrid book and a naffer-than-naff movie.

I never saw the movie in question. So why, you may well ask, am I so sure that it's so indescribably dreadful? I'll tell you why. It's because I'm not in it.

Let's go back. Way back.

2003. *The Devil Wears Prada* hits the bookstores. I tried reading it, but decided that having sex with a dead relative was preferable and hightailed it off to the local cemetery. Don't get me wrong, I enjoy trash as much as the next person. However, I like my trash to be quality trash, by which I mean *Scruples* trash or *Valley of the Dolls* trash. Nuanced trash.

I found *TDWP* singularly lacking in nuance. The multifaceted Anna was reduced to an imperious coat-flinging tyrant, and—this is the most horrid part—the groovy, idiosyncratic fashion people I know and love were entirely missing from the landscape conjured by the author. Where were all the freaks and funsters?

The world of fashion has always given a hearty *willkommen bienvenue welcome* to all the misfits, kooks and original thinkers of the world. Fashion has always been a safe space, a *salon des refusés* for people who might otherwise be unemployed, institutionalized, or forced into street theater or stripping, or even fluffing. La Weisberger replaced those quirky eccentrics with a bunch of overachieving, conventional careerist bimbos.

As far as I am concerned, this is nothing short of a crime against humanity. Replacing the Faridas and Alek Weks and Vivienne Westwoods and Marina Schianos and Loulous and Bettys and Piaggis and Emma Hopes and Pam Hoggs and Lori Goldsteins and Bethann Hardisons and Coddingtons and Pat McGraths and Roxanne Lowits and Lynn Yaegers and Carines and Anna Dello Russos with a bunch of annoying sorority girls was a horrid thing to do. Why replace the extraordinary with the ordinary?

If you think I am a little overly critical, keep in mind that Ms. Weisberger's books have been so much more successful than mine. As a result, my comments may be tinged with freudenschade. (The opposite of schadenfreude, i.e., taking displeasure in the fortunes of others as opposed to the reverse.) I admit that I may, as a result, not be entirely objective. If you haven't read *TDWP,* do not let me deter you. You might like it. Millions did.

A year or two after the unimaginably successful publication of the book, I got a call from a bubbly movie-production person. She was casting for the big-screen version of *The Devil Wears Prada*.

"Would you like to come in and read for the part of Nigel?" she asked.

Suddenly my disdain for the book melted like so much Velveeta. Please keep in mind that we fashion folk are not known for our consistency. In addition to which, I would ask you to remember what Gore Vidal said: "Never decline invitations to have sex or to be on TV." I am quite sure the same applies to movies.

"Yes. Emphatically, yes," I replied, and hung up the phone.

I then let out a little shriek of delight. I grabbed my dog, Liberace, and told him that together we were going to claw our way to the top. It was *our* moment!

In the days running up to my audition, I experienced a bouncy, breezy confidence. This whole movie thing was clearly meant to be. I have always been an attention-seeking show-off.

The entertainment biz was a natural fit for my "talents." I could not believe I had to wait this long! In addition to which, my inclusion in the movie would be a righting of wrongs. The book might have lacked nuanced, freaky fashion folk, but the movie would not, because . . . the movie would have *moi*!

Did I have any misgivings about being able to act?

Are you kidding?

I have always thought of movie acting as an absolute doddle. The notion that it's hard to imitate the actions and mannerisms of others seems laughable to me. You just need to be a ham, a mimic. Child actors are great because they understand this. Sorry, Meryl and George and Angelina! Love you, but is it really *that* hard?

Stage acting? That's a whole other story. Charging around a conventional theater stage in front of a live audience, trying to remember the part of King Lear, knowing that tomorrow night you have to play Othello, seems, indeed, like an impressive feat. But movie acting? Standing about on a set belching out your lines two or three at a time, take after take? Surely even I could manage that. And in this particular case—I refer to the role of Nigel—it seemed as if all I would have to do is play a gay fashion dude . . . myself.

Let's talk about Nigel. As those of you stoic souls who actually got through the book without committing suicide will recall, Nigel was the fey creative director of the fictitious *Runway* magazine. A consoling island in a sea of abuse, Nigel doled out sage advice to the beleaguered heroine.

Another cliché. The helpful homo.

Portraying a helpful homo would require a certain amount of

research and some effort. Why? Because I do not really possess that helpful *Queer Eye* homo gene. Never have.

Not only am I not particularly helpful, I am actively unhelpful. I have discovered over the years that the advice that I give is, in fact, quite reckless and confusing.

When people ask me for pointers, especially style advice, I find it really hard to restrain myself from making anarchic suggestions. If an advice seeker confesses to me that she needs a new look, I might well respond as follows: "Buy yourself an electric blue silk-satin trench coat, dye your hair blue-black—or better yet, buy a blue stripper wig—and then go home and toss out all your other clothes. In cold weather, think snake-skin unitard. You have an okayish body. Why not?"

Advice seeker: "Are puffy jackets still in?"

Moi: "No! Do not even think of leaving the house this season unless you are wearing a Miss Marple cape. Start wearing dove gray spats . . . and a monocle."

My advice, as you can see, is almost like a form of Tourette's. If some innocent gal asks for a beauty tip, I am quite likely to say something like "Top and bottom lashes. Seven days a week." Or: "Run home and plunge your breasts into ice-cold water."

Inspirational? Possibly. Helpful? Never.

Back to *Prada*.

Putting aside these minor misgivings over my ability to imbue Nigel with the requisite helpfulness, I decided to *go for it*.

I unfurled the exciting news about this big Hollywood breakthrough in one of my weekly phone conversations with my eighty-year-old dad, Terry. Before flitting off to heaven, he resided in an English seaside old folks' home in Brighton, England.

His response was characteristically skeptical.

"They called *you*. Goodness me, they must really be scraping the barrel."

When it comes to unconditional support, Terry was always the wind beneath my wings.

Buried somewhere 'neath Terence Sydney Doonan's naysaying incredulity, there was a legitimate point. What, indeed, were they thinking? Why cast an F-lister like me, whose screen credits are limited to random appearances on *America's Next Top Model* and VH1's *I Love the '80s* series, to play scenes opposite Oscar-laden Meryl Streep? Wasn't this surely a risky strategy?

I concluded that they must have decided to sprinkle some "real people" throughout the movie to add flava and brushed aside any misgivings. It was too late to turn back and too late for any kind of rational thought. I was entranced by the lights of Tinseltown. Like a moth to a flame, I was already hurtling toward my wing-singeing doom.

Adopting the kind of anything-for-kicks enthusiasm that made Barbara Stanwyck such a popular presence on every soundstage, I diligently learned my lines and showed up bright eyed, bushy tailed and embarrassingly early for my scheduled script reading. Delivering what I considered to be an appropriately pastiche-drenched characterization of a gay fashionista, I minced about and windmilled my arms. I vamped and camped. I poofed it up. I gave good nelly.

Smiling from ear to ear, the casting director informed me that I was utterly fabulous and begged me to come back and meet the director. She then handed me the entire screenplay and instructed me to learn huge chunks of it.

Wow! Lights! Camera! Action!

I set about committing the dialogue to memory. This was far more difficult than I would have imagined. And, for some strange reason, the dumbest chunks of text were the hardest. I'm talking about simple phrases like "Oh, hello!" "Good morning to you too," and "Well, I don't see why not. In fact, I'd love to!"

For some reason these fleeting snatches of dialogue were so much harder to memorize than more complicated sentences. I began to understand how Marilyn Monroe could, while lensing *Some Like It Hot,* have repeatedly and famously fucked up the line "Hello. It's me, sugar." It kept coming out "Hello, sugar! It's me!" or variations thereof. After take thirty, Billy Wilder had the line written on a blackboard. She required nearly fifty takes before getting it right.

As I struggled through the memorization of my lines, I had horrible visions of buggering up my takes and testing the patience of my costars. Anna Wintour was no longer haunting my dreams. Instead, I saw Meryl sighing and rolling her eyes and morphing into Mommie Dearest.

But I persevered. I was determined not to screw up my big chance. I was determined not to let Hollywood eat me alive. I would avoid the pitfalls of booze and dope and narcissism. I would be *professional.*

By the time I went back to meet Mr. Frankel, the director, I had committed my lines to memory. I had also convinced myself that stardom, popping champagne corks and a floor-length mink were all just a short limo ride away.

Sparkle, Neely, sparkle!

The day of the screen test arrived. I knocked it out of the

park. I made love to the camera. I gave it my all. After I delivered my lines, a delighted Mr. Frankel quizzed me about various people at *Vogue*. And then he asks specifically about Ms. Wintour.

What is she really like? Is she as bitchy, tough and imperious as the Prada-toting devil of Weisberger's novel?

I tell him the truth. I tell him that Anna is straightforward, smart and highly professional. She is an incredible mother. She is extremely well liked by her staff. Demonic? I have never even heard her raise her voice and have yet to meet anyone who has. I conclude by telling him that Anna, in sharp contrast to the Weisberger creation, has achieved her position and her success by pragmatism, vision, clarity and hard work rather than Caligula-like intimidation. He visibly glazes over.

This is when I should have smelled a rat, or at least a moldy chinchilla. But I did not. I was blinded by my Neely dreams. I felt Tracy Flick–ish and buoyant about my audition. Clearly this movie would only benefit by the addition to the cast of a real fashion insider, and that would be me.

Skipping out of the casting office, I ran smack-dab into fellow telly-nelly fashionista Phillip Bloch. We're old pals, but this did not stop us from giving each other the evil eye.

You may not understand what I am about to say, but please believe me when I tell you that this encounter was very much the equivalent of Hattie McDaniel running into Butterfly McQueen outside the casting office for *Gone with the Wind*. We eyed each other suspiciously. *Don't steal my part, bitch!*

Barely masking a foaming sea of competitive feelings, we commiserate politely about the agony of memorizing lines and go about our business.

As I rode the bus home—I love the M2's "limited stops" route, which zooms straight down Fifth Avenue—I couldn't help fantasizing about the limousines in my future. After the film comes out, it will be impossible for me to ride public transport. In a way, I would miss being "one of the people." If I got the urge to ride the M2, I could always concoct a disguise of some description. Maybe a blue stripper wig would be enough . . .

The next day I ran into E!/Style/Bravo fashion diva Robert Verdi. He too had been called to audition. Same story. While kibitzing with Mr. Verdi, my Hollywood glamour haze started to evaporate. I was forced to ask myself some unpleasant questions.

Was there a pansy alive who has not read for this part? Had no fashion fag been left unturned?

I reassured myself that I had nothing to worry about. These other poofters would lose out to me, me, me, Norma Desmond. Why? Because of the accent. I am a Brit and Nigel was supposed to be English. Despite having lived in the United States since the late seventies, I still say "fortnight" and "knickers" with Brit-like regularity.

One morning soon afterward, I was pooping my dog on the sidewalk and ran into the gorgeous Candace Bushnell. She lives in my neighborhood. I was and am a fan of her oeuvre. Candace and I often chitty-chat while picking up dog poop. It's a bonding experience that allows for other certain frank conversations. On this particular day, Candace, for better or worse, delivered a heapin' helpin' of that straight talk.

I regaled her with tales of my imminent stardom. I told her

about the auditioning process. I even told her about the fierce competition for the role of Nigel.

She gave me a look.

Even through her massive Chanel glamour shades I could see that it was a highly skeptical look. It was a look that said, "Hey, Blanche! You've been had."

As I dropped Liberace's poop into the handy receptacle at the end of our block, the realization dropped on me. It dropped on me like a ton of remaindered copies of *TDWP*.

I was not going to get the part—and neither were any of my fellow nellies. The whole audition charade was nothing more than a carefully orchestrated piece of unpaid research. We gays had been dragged in to swish it up—on camera, no less—for the delectation of some precast, overpaid straight actor. This thespian would then create his characterization based on our uncompensated-for mincings.

These dark suspicions were confirmed when the movie began lensing, just days later, with Stanley Tucci playing the part of Nigel.

Despite having played such a key role in the genesis of this movie, I was surprised when no tickets were forthcoming to the premiere.

So, like the wicked fairy in *Sleeping Beauty* whose invite to the christening of Aurora somehow got lost in the mail, I had no other option than to place a curse on Mr. Frankel, Ms. Weisberger and their entire cheesy-ass, cultural-bar-lowering, mediocre venture. Break a leg, bitches!

Time is a great healer. By the time the blockbuster, curse-immune movie was breaking every record known to man and winning every award and garnering free frocks for all concerned, I found it within me to forgive and let the healing begin. I found it within me to ask, "What would Anna do?"

Anna would don her welder-size glasses, assume an expression of noblesse oblige and move on.

And that's exactly what I intend to do . . . no, really, I do.

the dream
crusher

NOW THAT I AM IN MY SIXTIES, a veteran of the fashion scene,
I find myself ranting frequently about the younger generation.
On the positive side, I find people in their twenties to be far more
sweet and altruistic than those of yore. When I was a whipper-
snapper, me and my playmates were catty, selfish and superficial. We were too busy ironing the ruffles on our pirate outfits to
read a newspaper and engage with global problems. Today, in
sharp contrast, every young person I encounter is trying to make
a difference, helping out at homeless shelters or supporting or-
phanages in AIDS-ravaged countries. It's a sweet thing.

On the downside, young people today would appear to be
cursed with a strong megalomaniacal streak. Overly focused on
professional and material success, they are desperate to claw
their way to the top while overlooking the importance of creativity and originality. They would rather spend time honing their
entrepreneurial skills than waste time developing an idiosyn-

cratic voice. Everybody wants to be a global brand. Nobody seems able to chillax. This seems like a horrible way to spend your youth.

Your twenties should be sophomoric and exploratory and fun. This is the time to pluck your eyebrows into strange satanic configurations, to change your name to Ariadne or Arbuthnot, and to wear a giant alarm clock on your head.

I look back on my late teens and twenties with a sense of delight. I traveled the globe. I impulsively emigrated. I put dead coyotes in shop windows. I dressed up as the queen of England and got paid to do so. I sold hand-painted T-shirts. I got arrested wearing a skirt. I was inappropriate and uncouth. I was glam rock. I was punk (lite). I was even new romantic.

Career? What career?

On the rare occasions when I tried to be sensible, to force the issue and get all grown up and serious, it always backfired.

One day, in the very early eighties, I was busily selling T-shirts out of the back of my truck next to a chicken-wire fence on Melrose and Edinburgh in West Hollywood. (Chicken wire is great for dangling wire hangers and displaying mucho merch.) A pal screeched to a halt and attempted what I realize in retrospect was a *vocational intervention*.

"You can't go on like this. I mean, just look at what you are doing. It's tragic. You have become a street vendor. At this rate, you'll end up working the Renaissance Fairs. You need to go to New York and get a rep and show your T-shirt collection on Seventh Avenue. You need to go see Bernie Ozer."

Bernie Ozer (né Ozersky) was a legendary force in the fashion world. An unofficial Garment District ambassador, Bernie was known as *the* trend forecaster. He was hugely fat and very wise and wore daringly patchworked shirts and colorful oversize hats. And Bernie was a gourmand. The way to his heart, so my pal told me, was to bring him a lemon cake from Miss Grace's bakery in West Hollywood.

So, with the fear that I would end up pouring mead while wearing an Elizabethan costume or jousting in some godforsaken medieval theme park reverberating in my psyche, I purchased that cake, grabbed my samples and headed to New York City.

The transcontinental conveyance of the lemon gateau was a nerve-racking experience. People kept jamming their Samsonite weekenders on top of it. I flew most of the way with Miss Grace sitting on my lap.

When I called Bernie's office and told his secretary that I had brought him a lemon cake, I was immediately given an appointment.

The next day I showed up at Bernie's *bureau de la mode* wearing shorts and one of my T-shirts. A little too informal? Listen, I had been kicking back in L.A. for several years, so it's a miracle I wasn't wearing a Speedo. I had my samples, and most important, that bloody lemon cake, and that's what counted . . . or did it?

Knock, knock.

Bernie's office was lacquered in seventies burgundy and filled with trendy brass and Lucite tchotchkes. He was seated behind a grandiose desk looking like a gay Sydney Greenstreet. I plonked the cake in front of him and stood back. We both stared at it as if it were an explosive device. I waited for a reaction. He gave a snort of resignation and then attacked.

"What do you care if I go into a fucking diabetic coma!" he barked good-naturedly, and tore open the Miss Grace box as if it contained crack cocaine.

The rest of the interview consisted of me skipping about showing my samples while he ate cake and stared at my bare legs. I don't blame him. I do have great legs. And they were even better when I was in my twenties.

The good news: Bernie did not go into a diabetic coma.

The bad news: I did not become a billionaire T-shirt czar. No two-thousand-piece order was forthcoming from Macy's or any-where else. I suspect that Bernie, in his infinite wisdom, identi-fied my limitations on sight. He could tell that I was not ready for big-time wholesaling and distribution. He could see that I was much more the chicken-wire type. Before I knew it, me and my legs and my samples were headed back to L.A. and several more years of obscurity.

My Bernie interview had one positive outcome. It helped me realize that timing is everything. You cannot propel your career forward faster than it wants to go. This does not mean you have to waste your time. Not at all. When you are young, you simply need to throw a bunch of fabulosity against the wall and see what sticks. Work hard, stay positive and when a good opportunity floats into view, don't procrastinate, grab it with both paws as if it were a lemon cake.

During my twenties, I had no problem collaging together an income, albeit a modest one. (My W-2 for 1979 shows the princely sum of $5,175.00.) I worked in sales. I designed wacky theater sets. I schlepped for a photographer named Beverly Parker who shot country-and-western stars, thereby enjoying trips to Nashville, where I got to hang out with folks like Rosanne Cash and blind Ronnie Milsap and stuttering Mel Tillis. I also did odd jobs on movie sets, the most notable of which was designing the gallery set on *Beverly Hills Cop*.

Catastrophic sidebar: Prepping and shooting this movie took almost a year. When it came time to pay me, the Paramount accountant asked if I wanted cash or "points." The skeptic in me became convinced that they were trying to hoodwink me out of some deserved shekels. Because I was a total fucking naïve idiot and had no idea what "points" meant, and was much too stupid to ask around and find out, I opted for cash. The movie went on to break all box-office records known to man. It made so much money that it saved Paramount from the brink. If I had taken the points, I would now be lolling in a chateau in the south of France mainlining Beluga caviar and guzzling crème de menthe. (And probably looking like Bernie Ozer.)

After shooting at Paramount Studios, I had lots of fantasies about a career in movie-set design. I felt sure that a screen credit on such a major movie would open up a cavalcade of opportunities . . . and yet, there I was, back at the chicken-wire fence a few weeks later, collaging together my Frieda Freelance lifestyle.

In my early thirties I had a sobering realization: It was time to go work somewhere where I could get medical insurance and a bit of stability. But work where, doing what and for whom?

I had many strings to my bow, but window display seemed to

present the most opportunities. And so, at the age of thirty-four, I finally hung up my gypsy espadrilles and took a full-time job running the Barneys New York display studio.

What's my point? My point is that your twenties are the time to fluff and finagle. Fill this period with a creative mishmash of odd jobs and wacky interests. Untie your mind from your behind and cultivate it. Everything will eventually fall into place. There are so many opportunities. Now more so than ever.

The fashion world today is an exploding cornucopia of opportunity, or "opportunitay" as I like to think of it, since adding an "ay" makes it sound less corporate and more fun and Ru Paul–ish.

Sashay! Chantay! Opportunitay!

There have never been more fashion-related jobs than there are now. And it's only increasing. The universe of La Mode seems to double in size every year.

If you are a scrappy young gay or gal or guy or trans person and you cannot get some kind of entry-level schlepper freelance gig or full-time foothold in this vast terrain of design, public relations, sales, mags, blogs, pattern making, zip resourcing, rolling-rack pushing, wholesale, retail, schmetail, then you need to give your own boottay a good hard smack, possibly using a fly swatter in order to reach it.

Despite the plethora of low-hanging fruit and dingly-dangly opportunitays, many young saplings are floundering. This is because they insist on going about things ass-backward. While I, back in the day, had absurdly low expectations, the youngsters du jour now have stratospherically high ones. Impatient and grandiose, their goal is to start at the top. They seem to have no intention of paying their chicken-wire dues. Their heads are filled with unachievable accomplishments, unrealistic delusions, premature derangements, overly ambitious schemes and unattainable fantasias.

Blame it on *Project Runway.*

Thanks to Tim Gunn, Heidi and the gang, kids across America are suffering from the insane misconception that the only way to get involved in fashion is to establish *your own design house,* and that anything less than that constitutes a gruesome failure. Yes, YOU shall have your name on the door, and YOU shall have your own runway show, and YOU shall be the next Tom Ford, and YOU shall be a star!

There is only one person who can set them straight . . .

Enter THE DREAM CRUSHER (c'est moi!).

Now that I am a senior member of the fashion firmament, my mission in life is to tell these young people the cold, unvarnished truth. In this age of self-esteem building and entrepreneurial precociousness, this has become a massive undertaking. As fast as I can crush their dreams, somebody is building them back up again. Kids today are drenched with relentless positivity on a daily basis. Nobody seems willing to tell it like it is.

The truth is that most of us are lucky if we can simply claw our way to the middle.

Most people, me included, are far better suited to work for somebody else rather than inaugurate an eponymous brand or fashion label, especially when they are right out of college. One in a million fashionistas has the nuts and the gnads and the ovaries and the ideas and the shekeltastic infrastructure to become a Wang or a Raf or a Dries or a Miuccia. The vast majority of us do better in a support capacity. In other words, most of us are a gusset or a bust dart. Few of us have what it takes to become the gown itself. Few of us could handle big-time success if it came along, never mind attain it in the first place.

If, perchance, success arrives before maturity and experience, it will really do a number on you. You will morph into a strangely unappealing individual. You will resemble those people who win the lottery and go totally bat-shit. Yes, you will be wearing a mauve ostrich-skin jumpsuit and driving a matching mauve Maybach, but will you be happy?

In my role as dream crusher, I am obliged to divest the kids of today of their grandiosity. This role was thrust upon me inexplicably and mysteriously. I accept it. I inhabit it. I crush. But I also nurture.

The role of the dream crusher goes way beyond merely crushing dreams. I always make sure that I replace every crushed dream with an achievable goal. This process involves the delivery of a twinkly perfect nugget of advice—advice which, I might add, is desperately needed.

Example 1: A young gal accosts me on line at Starbucks.

"You are Mr. Fashion and I want to be a model."

"How tall are you?"

"Five feet . . . almost."

"It's never going to happen."

"Why?"

"You are twelve inches too short. And so am I."

"Fuck you!"

"Glad I was able to help. If you like the world of modeling, why not try for a gofer job at a modeling agency and work your way up? In ten years' time you could be office manager or even an agent. I'll have a venti Earl Grey tea, please. Bag on the side."

Example 2: A young lad stops me on the street and asks to show me his line of ornate ladies' hats. Before I can answer, he begins to show me samples and pictures. They look cute. He asks my opinion of his prospects. I give it to him.

"You need to radically modify your expectations. This can never be more than a hobby."

"Why?"

"Because hats are a minuscule category in fashion, an endangered species. Look around. No women are wearing hats, which means that no women are buying hats. In the 1930s women never left the house without a hat. Now it is rare to see a hat unless you are at an English garden party or a Southern Baptist church. And since you live in Brooklyn, you need to reconsider, regroup and restrategize."

"I know all that! [Getting annoyed.] But I am going to create a revolution. I am going to teach women to appreciate hats again."

"No, you're not. And here's why: American women are committed to their hair. *Fully committed!* They spend all their money having it straightened, augmented, braided, combed out and woven, and they currently show no inclination to cover it up with elaborate concoctions, except on rare occasions."

"Thanks for crushing my dreams."

"You are so welcome. Why not try scarves? They are a huge category and there are no sizing issues. Or better yet, go to beauty school and learn to do hair. Have a nice day."

While most kids today are well served to have their dreams crushed and replaced by more achievable goals, there are a small number of individuals who are not. They are the exceptions, the geniuses. While most of us are better suited to blunder about and baby-step our way through life, these talented supernovas are hitting the big time right out of the cradle.

These exceptions to the rule—the Proenza Schoulers, the Lims, the Thakoons, the Lams, the Prabals and the Altuzarras—are a delightfully, splendidly competent bunch, likable and hard-working too. They have pitched themselves into the pressure cooker of fashion and bravely endure operational, financial and emotional challenges which would probably have plunged the likes of me into a booze-addled abyss. And they are succeeding. No chicken-wire fences or abortive lemon-cake deliveries for them.

Admirable though I find these overachieving prodigies, I do have one tidgy-widgy criticism.

These fashion designers are a little too . . . self-effacing.

The reason for this is quite simple. The young designers of today are all, consciously or unconsciously, basing their public image on the enigmatic Garbo of fashion, namely Martin Margiela. Remote and unknowable, Margiela crafted one of the most mysterious and arty personas ever to have inhabited the fashion asylum. As a result, everyone secretly wants to be him.

Back in the last century, I once blithely snapped a picture of Martin while he was chatting with my colleague at the time, Ronnie Newhouse. This caused a *scandale fou*. Nobody is ever allowed to snap Monsieur Margiela. I was subsequently chased around the whitewashed showroom by admonishing Margiela acolytes in white couture lab coats. I was only allowed to keep the film in my camera on one condition: I had to promise to give the picture to Ronnie. La Newhouse was an early supporter of Martin's and he had a soft spot for her.

So, the goal of these young designers is to emulate that mysterious press-phobic Belgian legend. Ask them a direct question and their little toes point inward in an idiotic show of faux humility. They have yet to realize that this kind of ever-so-humble behavior, while it worked for Mr. Margiela, is almost the exact opposite of what we really want from them.

What do we want from them?

We want fabulosity, by which, of course, I mean we want the fabulosity of a great fashion impresario, a Chanel, an Oscar de la Renta, an Yves Saint Laurent.

I would love to teach classes in fabulosity, but my obligations as a dream crusher—*the* dream crusher—consume all my free time.

In the absence of my teachings, I have enlisted the help of three legendary designers. (Unbeknownst to these dudes, I channeled their thoughts while in a deep trancelike state.) None are humble. Each one has a distinct identity or persona. Each designer's lesson addresses a different aspect of fabulositay.

LESSON #1. *Valentino's guide to pug management*

Your private plane has landed. You rise from your seat with an air of grandeur and disdain. An assistant holds up a mirror for you to check your tan. It is perfect, which is not surprising since you just spent the last three weeks spread-eagled on the deck of your yacht, circling the island of Capri.

Doors to manual.

Another assistant places your cashmere coat over your shoulders. On go the Aristotle Onassis shades. You appear at the top of the steps and wave at the waiting paparazzi. A blizzard of flashbulbs. Ciao, Roma!

Then like Anita Ekberg in *La Dolce Vita*, you take two runs at it, darting back inside and emerging again, thereby ensuring that the paparazzi get plenty of shots.

You descend to a waiting limo while waving to your fans. You are, of course, followed by hundreds and hundreds and hundreds of pugs. So many pugs that nobody can figure out how on earth they all fit into that plane. (As Seth Meyers declared at the CFDA Awards in 2012, "Valentino is recovering from surgery. He had an extra arm surgically attached so that he can hold more pugs.")

This, young designers of today, is fabulositay at its finest!

You and the pugs slither into your limo and purr toward your palazzo, where you are greeted by four hundred liveried servants lined up outside in their starched pinafores, each clutching a geriatric pug. (The older ones stay at home when you travel.)

You swan into the great hall past a swirl of Tiepolos, Caravaggios and El Grecos. You sink into a squishy couch that was probably once owned by Pauline Bonaparte or Pauline de Rothschild, or some broad called Pauline, and are immediately engulfed by orchids, pugs and the intoxicating ambience which you have created using your wits, your creativity and your genius. You grab a pad and start sketching the fall line . . .

LESSON #2. *The Karl Lagerfeld guide to sartorial idiosyncrasy*

Achtung! When I, Herr Lagerfeld, was a young man, I *never* wore jeans and T-shirts. As a purveyor of luxury and dreams, I always went to great lengths to appear distinguished and glamorous. I was sporting those high Proustian collars and monocles even back in the seventies.

Today's young designers are less than impressive in the sartorial department. Why do they choose to dress like college students? Why do these attractive young men favor J.Crew T-shirts, Top-Siders and scuzzy jeans? Why would you be so willfully schlumpy and degagé when you could stalk the earth dressed like an eighteenth-century aristocratic vampire?

Every designer needs an iconic look. If the *South Park* boys cannot make a recognizable cartoon out of you, then you need to up the ante. You need a signature flourish, non?

LESSON #3. *The Azzedine Alaïa guide to social media (hash tag whybother?)*

Moi, Azzedine Alaïa, I have weathered the social-media revolution and emerged unscathed and profoundly indifferent. Le tweet? *Qu'est-ce que c'est?*

Not a tweet, nor a chirp nor a chirrup. Has it hurt moi? It would appear to have done the opposite. In those years when tweets and twats were allegedly so critical to any kind of success, my business has become larger than ever. For the women du monde, my frocks and shoes and bags are *l'addiction*.

You young designers are getting caught up and distracted by le social media. You spend your days smiling over positive comments and weeping at the negative ones. Maybe I am from l'old school, but there seems to me to be something deeply *tragique* about caring so much about what other people think. The frantic checking of phones seems so—*comment dire?*—embarrassing.

If you are hoping to establish yourself as a *grand chose* in the fashion world, then maybe it would be good to *suivez-moi* and cultivate a little Alaïa-esque hauteur and indifference. If your designs are good *maintenant*, think of how great they could be if you took all your social-media time and dedicated it to the act of creation. Women cannot wear tweets.

À tout à l'heure!

CLEARLY THIS CHAPTER has zigzagged all over the place. In recognition of the fact that the careers of younger readers may hinge on a clear understanding of what's been said, I offer the following recap.

Young people today are exceptionally caring and altruistic, but they are not having as much fun as they should because they are overly fixated on world domination and because they are not cross-dressing on a healthy regular basis.

Most people are not destined for megastardom. Most are better served to approach life, as I did, with a good work ethic but zero expectations. This guarantees that you will always be pleasantly surprised.

The young megastar designers of today are too schlumpy and humble. They need to gussy up, and they also need to spend more time making frocks and less time making tweets.

Lastly, and most important, please remember that transporting gooey cakes across state lines is inconvenient and can endanger the life of the recipient.

tom ford's
moist lip

TOM FORD IS THE ONLY PERSON I know who has successfully integrated the word "cunt" into a memorial speech. No mean feat. It happened when he was eulogizing the late and much-missed *New York Times* fashion journalist Amy Spindler.

Amy died too young and she knew it. Her natural feistiness was magnified by her cruel and horrible illness. Tom quoted the dying and irate Amy as saying, "Just because I have cancer does not mean I can't be a cunt."

Tom's speech caused a few raised eyebrows. I am not quite sure why. By being honest, he offered mourners a clear and touching reminder of Amy's tough, vibrant personality and an insight into her final struggle.

There are many other reasons why I love Tom.

He cuts a great suit. Having worked on Savile Row, I am a sucker for a bit of nifty tailoring.

His Tobacco Vanille perfume is intoxicating and makes me wish I smoked cigarettes again. Or maybe even a pipe.

I also love Tom Ford because Tom Ford loves a moist lip. I love a moist lip too. Who doesn't?

ONCE UPON A TIME I was planning a party for the launch of Mr. Ford's huge photographic retrospective monograph. In order to add a little sizzle to the occasion, I suggested to Lisa Schiek, Tom's PR guru, that we commission sugar cookies bearing an image of Tom's face and the words EAT ME knocked out in blocky white lettering, à la Ed Ruscha. These scrumptious goodies would be served to arriving guests along with a glass of champagne. We could also, budget permitting, stitch up a bunch of cushions bearing his image and the words SIT ON ME. "I'm sure Richard Avedon won't mind us taking his iconic portrait of Tom and using it to create TF souvenirs," I trilled, optimistically.

Lisa was less than enthusiastic. Her response was polite but adamant: instead of cookies and cushions, Tom would prefer us to focus our attention on the male servers. She said that Tom would like to see handsome model-slash-waiters holding drink trays. I received a follow-up memo with styling specifics: the lads should have "a moist lip, dewy cheek and a light tan, as if they had just spent a couple of hours lolling by the pool that very morning."

I was uneasy. While my EAT ME idea was, admittedly, a little too playful for the sophisticated Ford brand, Tom's alternative was rather nuanced. The entire concept was a minefield of subjectivity. One person's moist lip was another person's slobbery *bouche*. How moist was too moist? When was moist not moist enough? Was it better to be too moist than too dry? Regarding the cheek: What was the difference between dewy and plain old greasy?

"Return to your station, redew your cheeks and reapply your lip gloss, you lightly tanned, naughty, dry-lipped waiter," I could almost hear myself saying.

For reasons too complicated to enumerate, but most of which were budget related, I was unable to hire a phalanx of square-jawed Adonises for Tom's book launch. We were obliged instead to rely on the waiters from our own Barneys restaurant, none of whom had, as far as we could see, either a moist lip or dewy cheek, and most of whom were female. After scouring the kitchen, my team hit pay dirt: a nice-looking bloke with a light tan.

"You'll do!" we shrieked, and dragged the hapless victim off to the makeup department, where, much to his horror, we glossed his lip and dusted his cheek. We then shoved a drink tray in his hand.

Tom arrived. He glanced at our lone, lightly tanned dude in his ill-fitting white shirt and his seen-better-days schlumpy black pants, and he winced. He then sat down and began signing books for the around-the-block line of fans that had come to worship their idol.

Eventually, Tom habituated to the presence of his undewy, unmoist accomplice. They exchanged polite banter. Mr. Ford is a smart guy. He realized that I had done him a huge service. Why risk comparison with somebody younger, moister and dewier? How much better to have a blokey regular guy. How much better to have a *flattering adjacency*!

Sales recap: We sold about $50,000 worth of books, including tons of the $350 deluxe white leather-bound version.

Lipgate was, as it turned out, a good warm-up for my next encounter with Mr. Ford. Let us now move on from Tom's preoccupation with square jaws and moist lips, and head south to the world of grotty feet.

All of us think we have gorgeous feet, especially when we are young. I always thought mine were quite noteworthy: I see them as sturdy little Celtic hooves, perfectly in proportion with my gnomelike physique. My high insteps recall, at least to my eyes, those famous images of Rudolf Nureyev's appendages. (Avedon, *again!)*

Suddenly, a few winters ago, that all changed. I was skipping along the beach in Florida when I suddenly noticed that my right big toenail looked radically different. It bore a blotch the color of scrambled egg. So perturbed was I by this development that I skipped to an abrupt halt. This is unusual. I am an enthusiastic skipper. Once I get going, I tend to keep right on skipping.

The following week, I skipped over to see my doctor, who diagnosed toe fungus and prescribed ciclopirox, a slow-acting but noninvasive antifungal nail lacquer. Determined to restore the rogue toenail to its former glory in time for my summer vacation, I applied the unguent with great diligence.

Despite my best efforts, the scrambled egg persisted. When it became apparent that the stubborn malady would be accompanying me and my Jonny on our trip to Capri, I zipped out and bought a pair of those hippie flip-flop-style Birkenstocks. Not very glamorous, but here's the deal: The toe-thong leather flap exactly covered the offending spot of fungus.

I also purchased a Ped Egg. This sleek little foot scraper, much advertised via late-night infomercials, was, at the time, sold as part of a tantalizing buy-one-get-one-free deal. The spare Ped Egg was immediately put to use, very successfully, as a Parmesan cheese grater. The very same design that catches those foul foot scrapings with such deathly efficiency works like a dream to accumulate finely shredded *fromage*. Just make sure you Magic Marker your Ped Eggs—Sharpie the word "hoof" onto the unsavory one—so they don't get mixed up.

I have always found this kind of freewheeling functionality to be very stylish. What could be chicer than drying freshly rinsed silk panties in a lettuce spinner kept for this very purpose under your bathroom sink? This kind of lateral thinking was first revealed to me some three decades ago when I worked at that suburban John Lewis department store, where a colleague—the head girdle saleslady—used a pair of plastic salad servers to subdue any uncooperative fleshy pouches that erupted during the trying on of corsets and other foundation garments.

Meanwhile, back in Capri.

Despite the toenail fungus, Jonny and I are having a luscious time. Capri is a great place for skipping. Thanks to my Birkenstocks, my affliction goes unnoticed by the international glitterati. Until . . .

Out of the blue, we receive an unexpected invitation to dine with the velvet mafia aboard an extremely long yacht. Whose yacht? I refuse to name names. As you can tell, I am a very sensitive, private person who would never divulge the details of his personal life.

The truth is I don't want to annoy the velvet mafia by blabbing too much. If they became annoyed, they might break my kneecaps, and then I could no longer skip. However, I will tell you this: To skip from one end of this particular boat to the other would take at least twenty minutes.

If there is one thing I know about the velvet mafia, they all get regular pedicures. So I prepped for the occasion by Ped Egging my tootsies, sloshing on an extra layer of ciclopirox and donning my Birkenstocks.

But my cunning preparations were all in vain. When we arrived at said boat, we were—horror of horrors—*immediately told to remove our shoes*!

Cocktails on the poop deck!

"What the hell is wrong with you," hissed my Jonny a few minutes later. "You look like Ratso Rizzo with his gimpy leg." I looked at my reflection in an adjacent lacquered wall. (Yes, the velvet mafia lacquers the walls of their pleasure boats, that's how velvety it gets.) One leg was pretzeled awkwardly around the other, my left foot mashing onto my right foot in an unsuccessful effort to conceal the grotesque digit.

And suddenly—Ciao! Dolce vita! Arrivederci, Roma!—there's Tom.

Tom Ford, fresh from the triumphant opening of his severely chic new store in Milan, is lounging on a mound of cushions and he's talking eyebrows. Eyebrows! Eyebrows! Eyebrows!

He takes no interest in my afflicted toe. He only has eyes for my eyebrows, and everybody's eyebrows. Eyebrows, it quickly becomes apparent, are his new canvas. He has moved on from the moist lip and is now devoting himself to a tenacious pursuit of the perfect tweeze.

The handsomely browed Mr. Ford is, as it turns out, a font of tips and information about the improvement and shaping of brows. He vehemently cautions my Jonny, a gritty potter who has never even thought much about his eyebrows, against sloppy dye jobs and overtweezing.

Suddenly, and without warning, Tom ditches the eyebrow seminar. He grabs me and begins to physically deconstruct my outfit. I permit him to restyle me. First, he's Tom Ford, so why not? Second, if he's focusing on my outfit, at least he won't be looking at my toenail.

Tom is of the opinion that I look much too uptight and "tucked in." I am sure he is right. I have never been good at doing the rumpled *sauvage* look. I was born mod. I came of age in a mod world. I will die mod, and we mods don't do degagé. We do neat. In addition to which I think the rumpled look only works if you are tall and tanned, and have a moist lip and a dewy six-pack. On a short, dry-lipped person such as myself, messy looks tradge.

Despite my protestations, Tom is determined to crease up my shirt and pull it out of my pants, and maybe even tie the two front shirttails into a sassy knot. This is not easily accomplished since I have painstakingly tucked my shirttails neatly inside my underpants. Okay, I know that's a seriously naff thing to do, but that's just how I am. I need to know that my shirt will remain in place no matter how much skipping I do.

So Tom is yanking my shirt—hard, very hard. Somehow he also has hold of the waistband of my underpants. Elastic is straining. Buttons are flying. Beads of sweat are accumulating.

"Tom! Leave him alone!" yells Tom's lovely boyfriend,

Richard Buckley, adding, somewhat disconcertingly, "Maybe he likes the way he looks!"

But Tom keeps on *sauvaging* me. The more he yanks, the more my underpants ride up.

Suddenly, I realize the full horror of my situation: Tom Ford is giving me a wedgy in front of the entire velvet mafia. It's only a matter of time before one of them notices my toe. 'Ere long I shall be walking the velvet plank.

Valentino, swathed in linen and pastel cashmere and clearly enjoying his well-deserved retirement with unapologetic Italian élan, clocks my fungalicious tootsie and freezes.

He shudders. He closes his eyes and clutches imaginary pearls.

I am totally busted. All eyes are on my hideous toe. Including Tom's.

Val then turns his gaze across the Med toward the hilltop ruins of the villa where the Emperor Tiberius—perverted, herpes-encrusted and hideous—lived out his final sordid years.

Val's gesture was a salutary reminder to all of us that there is always someone more grotty, more leprous than oneself.

toxins are the new cargo pants

BACK IN THE 1950s, stylish girls would do anything to achieve that rail-thin, society-bitch, Babe Paley silhouette. It wasn't enough to torture your innards into a long-line girdle, you also needed a little helper, or, more specifically, a tapeworm. This was the midcentury version of a gastric bypass. You were no-body unless you had your own live-in parasite.

If you think this is grotesque, then hang on to your gizzards. There is stuff going on today which makes all that tapeworm swallowing of yesteryear seem positively cutesy. The history of fashion and food, and the relationship between the two, is both fascinating and disturbing. Every decade I have observed new foodie fads and disorders arrive on the scene, searing the gorges and scraping the bowels of every fashion person in their path, and every decade things get more insane . . .

Let's get the gnarliest trend out of the way first. I am not going to sugarcoat it for you. I am just going to come right out and say it: There are fashionable people walking among us who are *drinking their own urine*. There, I've said it.

Unsurprisingly, this particular fad first reared its head in the late sixties when hippies spent their spare time sitting in orgone* boxes, drilling holes in one another's heads—it's called trepanning—and swallowing extremely long rags, all at the insistence of their hollow-eyed yogis. It was an all-bets-are-off era of consciousness-raising, experimentation and, yes, urine drinking.

The goal of drinking your own pee? Mental clarity, spiritual and physical well-being and, last but not least, beauty. Among the notables who gave it a whirl was J. D. Salinger. You could say he liked to take the piss out of himself.

The great hippie revival started at the end of the twentieth century and continues today. Caftans, communes, organic food co-ops, greenmarkets and music festivals all came back into vogue, and so did . . . gulp . . . urine drinking. Convinced of the health and beauty benefits of this transgressive activity, style mavens began enthusiastically partaking of their own piddle on a daily basis.

I became fascinated by the return of this taboo-busting practice. In a desperate attempt to understand the phenomenon, I sought out and interviewed several fashionable guzzlers. I wanted to get inside their heads, if not their bladders.

"I'm a devotee," a magazine editor told me on condition of the strictest anonymity, "and I never get colds. My Japanese

---

* See the great counterculture documentary titled *W.R.: Mysteries of the Organism*.

uncle taught me how to get the best results, but it's not the subject of dinner-party chat. It's between me and my pee."

"It's healing and cleansing and, yes, I think it's really catching on," said a fashion consultant and stylist. "If you do drugs or booze, you can taste it the next day. I'm very careful about who I tell. If word got out, I could never show my face at the Four Seasons again."

Others were more out and proud.

"What's the big deal?" said New York–based photographer Johnny Rozsa. "Urine therapy has been around for so long and the benefits are so well documented. I'm not a golden-shower queen: I started doing it to help my psoriasis. During that period, I noticed my skin was like a baby's bottom—a clean one, I might add. People think of piss as dirty, they associate it with poop. What I've discovered, along with many others—including Gandhi and Lal Bahadur Shastri—is the pure magic of pee. It's mostly urea, which has so many gorgeous properties!"

Mr. Rozsa grudgingly admitted that "the whole thing is a bit of a palaver," adding, "You see, you have to drink the middle pee when you wake up."

Middle pee?

"You pee out the first bit, then clench, then pee into a glass, clench again and pee the rest down the toilet. I add apple juice to the 'middle' urine and gulp it down."

After encountering all these rabidly pro-urine opinions, I started to wonder why I was not giving it a whirl.

Fortunately, just in the nick of time, I happened upon a balanced assessment of urine drinking written by a bloke named Robert Todd Carroll. He lays out the pros and cons in a straightforward manner, ultimately labeling it a fairly harmless practice. Pee is, after all, 95 percent water; the rest is nitrogenous waste from the liver, including a few excess minerals and nutrients that might get absorbed if you gave them a second chance. His conclusion? "As a daily tonic, there are much tastier ways to introduce healthful products into one's bloodstream." Mr. Carroll does, however, highly recommend drinking pee "for those rare occasions when one is buried beneath a building or lost at sea for a week or two."

Less cringe making than urine drinking, but no less incomprehensible, is the new mania for eating raw. Yes, fashion folk are hanging up their pots and pans for good. The raw-food trend is, even as I write, sweeping the alimentary canals of the modishly spiritual.

The original hippies were always much too busy skipping through the glades of Golden Gate Park to be bothered with elaborate culinary preparations. It was inevitable that they would go raw. As with urine drinking, the revival of all things counterculture has triggered fresh interest in the whole notion of *not cooking*.

I was made aware of the raw-food revival by my old pal designer John Bartlett. He adopted this diet after a trip to the Tree of Life Rejuvenation Center in Patagonia, Arizona, where he'd gone to do battle with what he called his "toxic mucus buildup."

"It accumulates in our intestines and colon, and then diseases get trapped," explained John, adding, "So I went there to eat raw and cleanse myself completely."

The raw-food rage, as practiced by John, has two basic rules: First, eat a vegan (nothing from an animal) diet, and, second, never turn on the stove. Cooking is evil because it destroys the food's enzymes. Et voilà! A raw cucumber lasagna! Bon appétit!

Mr. Bartlett denies any candy-bar lapses. He does, however, enjoy a few quick puffs on an American Spirit, the preferred cigarette of the fashion woo-woo set.

Stylish American Spiritualists are often to be seen lighting up—and hacking up toxic mucus—outside Quintessence, a restaurant on East Tenth Street. With an additional catering service in Manhattan, the Quintessence mini-empire is the epicenter of the New York raw lifestyle.

Upon Mr. Bartlett's recommendation, I spent an evening at the Tenth Street location and quizzed the regulars to find out what, other than a fear of disease-laden mucus, was behind this bizarre trend.

"It's such a big movement—*literally*!" chuckled fashion consultant Robert Forrest, while chewing on a Quintessence sun burger. "Delicious. It's made from sunflowers and flax seeds and other stuff," raved the healthy-looking sixtyish executive. "I never travel without them."

While most diners shared Mr. Forrest's positive feelings about their meal, a few neophytes could be heard losing patience as they waited for their food.

"If it's all raw, then what's taking so long?" kvetched one rag & bone–clad female, not unreasonably.

"The chef is massaging your kale. Yes, boiling would be quicker, but it kills all the enzymes," chirped the waitress.

All this talk of kale massaging gave me a sense of urgency. I had no intention of waiting until the wee hours while the chef harangued my snap peas into edibility. Time to order.

The menu consisted mostly of ingenious quote-swaddled facsimiles of regular cooked meals (e.g., "pasta" and "shrimp wonton"). I ordered the "burrito" and found it light and quite bearable, if a little heavy on the avocado.

For dessert, I tucked into Mr. Bartlett's favorite dessert, a "mudslide." This strange triple-decker fantasia consisted of pecan, carob, dates, mesquite powder, coconut and—hello, again!—avocado.

I fired probing questions at the now replete Mr. Forrest about the specific benefits of the diet. He mumbled something about "releasing toxins," ordered a couple of sun burgers to go for his upcoming trip to Dubai and left.

What's it all about, alfalfa? Why are fashion people so fixated on toxins and the vanquishing thereof? Is it a metaphor for self-loathing or just a passing fad?

I scrutinized the menu for clues and found the following screed: "We believe that by eating uncooked food long enough, we will regain the fifth element and the mystical powers of our ancestors."

I resolved to cut through the mucus once and for all and get the real story. I called the Quintessence HQ. I tracked down one of the three owners, a Chinese lady who goes by the *Lord of the Rings*–ish name of Tolentin Chan. Miss Chan was less than keen to talk about that "fifth element" or her ancestral mystical powers. She was, however, a lot clearer about the overall benefits of raw food than some of her Seventh Avenue clients.

"I ate a standard American diet, and my health was terrible," said Tolentin, who in her pre-raw days suffered from asthma, thyroid problems and continuous colds. "Starch and dairy had coated my lungs with mucus."

Now, thanks to raw food, Tolentin enjoys an asthma-free life. Her health issues now are stress-related: running a restaurant without the profit margins from liquor sales is working her nerves. Why no booze?

"Alcohol creates yeast, so we can't sell it. We are not making a lot of money, but it's okay. My motive is to share my knowledge about enzymes."

Enzymes?

"A high-enzyme diet will rejuvenate the body, energize you and make you feel like a newborn." According to Tolentin, aging is synonymous with a reduction in metabolic and digestive enzymes. Raw food replaces these enzymes.

Suddenly, I realized why the fashion flock has embraced the raw lifestyle. *Mucus, schmucus! Toxins schmoxins!* It's all about vanity. The raw craze is nothing more than a smoke screen for that age-old quest for eternal youth.

Now I remembered something John Bartlett said regarding his Arizona retreat. "The guy who runs this place is sixty and looks thirty-five!" No wonder Alicia Silverstone and the *Playboy* Barbi Twins have gone raw!

WITHIN THE FASHION ASYLUM, foodie fads come and go faster than a chicken vindaloo flies through a senior citizen. Urine guzzling and raw food are now waning in popularity. They have been eclipsed by a sinister, plaguelike phenomenon.

I'll never forget the first time I saw one of those freaky,

sinister, dark green *things*. It was sitting on somebody's desk in the Barneys corporate office. And then the next day I saw another one and another. It was like *Invasion of the Body Snatchers*. Every time we had a meeting, more of these mysterious objects would appear.

"It's a mixture of seaweed, plankton, wheatgrass and vitamins."

"But you seem to be drinking nothing else."

"It takes seven days. I'm on a cleanse."

"Why? What's it supposed to do?"

"I'm getting rid of all my toxins."

(Here we go again!)

"What's a toxin?"

"I'm not sure . . ."

"You look great."

"I've lost seven pounds. My goal weight is 105 pounds."

"You will look like a cadaver."

"Hopefully, soon."

The fashion world has embraced "the cleanse" with a vengeance. Here, finally, is a socially acceptable way to ensure that you get all your vitamins and minerals while maintaining the terrifyingly low body weight of a Ukrainian fashion model. And, as if that isn't fabulous enough, you will also be ridding yourself of all those toxins, whatever the hell they are.

Gradually the cleanse has proliferated—kombucha, mandrake, aardvark spittle, celery, kumquat and aloe—and the absence of a sludge-filled bottle is now more noteworthy than its presence. It is important to note, however, that the cleanse has yet to achieve global acceptance. There are wicked toxic hold-outs and some really naughty pockets of resistance.

A couple of years back . . .

Julie Gilhart, the former fashion director of Barneys, and I had scheduled a lunch meeting with three female execs from the House of Lanvin who were in town from Paris to discuss plans for Alber Elbaz's tenth anniversary as designer for the house.

Julie was stuck in traffic so the girls and I went ahead and ordered.

"Steak frites."

"Moi aussi."

"Make zat trois."

Françoise, Solange and Brigitte all ordered the fattiest thing on the menu, and I chose a lesbian lentil salad.

Françoise, Solange and Brigitte rolled their eyes at my healthy choice and then ordered a vat of *vin rouge* to wash down their steak frites.

Julie arrived in a flurry of air kissing and apologies. She sat down, rummaged in her Balenciaga bag and pulled out—you guessed it!—a plastic bottle containing what looked like green bile.

"Qu'est-ce que c'est?" whispered Françoise.

Waving away the menu politely, Julie announced that she was "on a cleanse" and would not be eating. She unscrewed the top of her lichen-and-beet-and-bergamot bowel purge, or some such thing, and began slugging it back.

"Pourquoi?" asked Solange.

"I need to release my toxins."

The three Frogs looked at one another.

"Les américaines, elles sont vraiment folles, non?" opined Brigitte, and forked a juicy slice of steak into her *bouche*.

Conclusion: As insanely specific as foodie fads and disorders are within the fashion universe, there are important regional differences. Yanks are terrified of toxins. Frogs thrive on them. And Brigitte, Françoise and Solange all lit up as soon as we hit the sidewalk.

thom browne's hairy ankles

A MASH-UP OF GENDER-CONFUSED fascist lesbianism. A shrunken preppy jacket with an armpit-scraping, high-waisted pant. Howdy Doody taken to his complete and utter lunatic conclusion. Visconti's *The Damned* meets Pasolini's *Salo*. Lacroix meets von Trapp. Liberace meets Hitler. Gilbert & George meet Ross Perot. White mink stoles, calf-length skirts, marcel-waved hair, fur-trimmed capes, cashmere stockings and Swarovski-encrusted attaché cases . . . and that's just the men.

The above are some random notes I took while watching a recent Thom Browne menswear show.

How did Thom happen? How did he become the most influential menswear designer of the 2000s while simultaneously being the most unbridled and avant-garde and totally fucking crazy?

During the eighties, and most of the nineties, men's designer clothing was huge. And by huge, I do mean capacious, tentlike, flowing, ample. If you were a trendy dude who wandered into Maxfield, Barneys or Charivari, then you saw immediately that cocoons and capes and general bagginess were where it was at. If a guy wanted a black Yohji highwayman's cloak, a billowing Versace scarf-print silk shirt or a black boxy boiled-wool Comme des Garçons suit—those voluminous CDG suits were Karl Lagerfeld's preferred uniform before he dropped major poundage on that cornbread diet—he could have his pick.

The basic assumption was as follows: Designer clothes are expensive. Rich dudes tend to be well-fed and beefy. Et voilà! Blouson is the mot du jour!

If, on the other hand, you were freakishly undersized, or just poor and petite, then you were shit out of luck.

I am one of those freakishly undersized personages. As a result, that baggy eighties Bananarama blousy period was, for me, a very emotionally scarring one. Being surrounded by designer clothing and not fitting into any of it was an alienating and horrific experience. Once in a while I would give it a whirl. I would try on a Montana this or an Armani that. The result? I was so swamped by fabric that I was invariably mistaken for an oven mitt. People would pick me up, stuff their hands inside me and slam me upside their pot roasts.

My point is this: The oversized ethos only worked on dudes of average or above-average height. So what *did* I wear?

Back then, back before LiLo and Kim and Perez and Al-Qaeda and Brangelina and Real Housewifery, there was no Zara or Uniqlo or H&M. There was no affordable fashion in teensy sizes. But my drive toward self-adornment was powerful. I found a way to survive: vintage clothing.

I came to know every good second-hand store in New York City, Miami Beach and Los Angeles. I sussed out the emporiums that always carried a meaty selection of unworn dead stock or secondhand merch and came away with armfuls of well-priced trouvays. The clothing manufacturers of the fifties, sixties and seventies were fully committed, back before the arrival of all that baggy blousonerie, to a niftier, narrower silhouette.

Before long, I became a rigorous vintage connoisseur. I could spot a moldy green armpit at fifty paces. I knew how to check seams for lice. And I would still be checking for skid marks and buying vintage if it were not for one man. His name is Thom Browne. With his shrunken ethos, Thom put the "dinky" back in designer clothing.

If you kidnapped Thom Browne from his home in New York City and plonked him down outside a convenience store in Kentucky, people would assume that he had escaped from the local mental health facility. His personal style is so codified and perversely conservative that it would definitely freak out the locals; with his high-waisted, flat-front pants; shrunken jackets; oversize pant cuffs cropped to expose several inches of ankle and hairy shinbone; and massive, cartoonish wing tips, Thom manages to simultaneously embody and destroy every menswear convention. His vision for men combines and magnifies various twentieth-century archetypes: the sixties congressman, the prewar Ivy Leaguer, Bobby Kennedy, Mr. Rogers and more.

Despite the objective weirdness of the TB look, it has been hugely influential. It is *the* influence. You cannot walk into a store today without seeing traces of Browne: ventriloquist-dummy-size jackets, a cardigan with a contrasting arm stripe, a painfully narrow tie, a center-vented gray wool jacket with a grosgrain ribbon trim.

When I happen to see Thom sitting in a restaurant or walking down the street, all Thom'd up, I usually think, *That's either Thom Browne or it's a very stylish and handsome Jehovah's Witness.* Thom is, in many ways, both. He creates and proselytizes the Browne look with a missionary zeal. He is a bloke with a vision and, unlike certain designers I could name who never seem to wear their own clothes—you know who you are!—he lives and breathes his own sartorial philosophy. His conviction and passion are what have propelled him into the spotlight. The courageous exaggerations of the Browne style, the polar opposite of the floppy draperie that dominated menswear for so long, have made him the most relentlessly copied menswear name to come along in years. He understood that the plump baby boomers and the eighties muscle dudes were aging out of their designer fixation, making way for a new generation of scrawny manorexics. A wave of hipster postgrunge freaks had arrived and they have no desire to look even remotely like an oven mitt. Their fashion icon was Spud from *Trainspotting.*

I don't do the supershort Thom Browne pant—my legs are short enough already—but I am nonetheless one of his acolytes. He has given me a way to look both tidy and eccentric. And—cue the trumpets and heavenly choirs—that quirky shrunken-jacket silhouette is, on my freakishly undersized body, a perfect fit. It looks *normal*! Praise the Lord!

And what of the man himself? Who is the dude behind the grosgrain?

A one-man performance troupe, Mr. Browne eats at the same

restaurants at the same time every day. I have no idea why. Despite having had many conversations with Thom, I have no idea what makes him tick, what it is like to *be* Thom and wander the streets with chilly ankles. He is well mannered but remote. This old-school reserve has only added to the enigma. Thom Browne the unknowable.

The depths of Thom's unknowability are confirmed every time he stages a fashion show. These occasions are dominated by outrageously unwearable concoctions—ballooning skirts, squishy cod pieces and linebacker shoulders—which challenge all of our preconceived notions about fashion. Men in terrorist masks and quasibridal frocks wander around rooms filled with turquoise wedding cakes. Chicks with giant silver egg-shaped thingys on their heads reposition themselves like giant chess pieces. What does it all mean? No explanatory notes are provided. Whether promoting men's clothing or women's, these arty, protracted, incomprehensible and thoroughly enjoyable affairs never reveal anything about this particular season's concept or about the man himself.

I love to watch the facial expressions of the show attendees. Without the benefit of explanatory insights into Thom's MO, the audience is suspended in a state of mild discomfort. Should we cheer? Are we allowed to laugh? Are these clothes for sale? Watching the mugs of the front-rowers at a recent show, I suddenly became aware that I had seen this particular expression somewhere before. It's the same embarrassed-but-slightly-concerned face I have seen on my neighbor's fluffy cat as she executes a poo in her litter box.

Of one thing I am certain, Thom is extremely anal-retentive

about the production of his shows. Rehearsals continue until everything is just so. I base this observation on the fact that Thom once kept the sobbing, bare-legged fashion pack waiting al fresco for half an hour in Arctic temperatures. Our tears were turning to icicles as we begged for mercy and pantomimed hypothermia to the PR flacks with clipboards who were observing our slow death with uncaring gazes through a frosty window. "Thom needs one more run-through," said a gray-clad acolyte and rebolted the door.

Last Christmas I walked into Il Cantinori, one of Thom's regular New York eateries. Near the window was a long table with sixteen gray-suited look-alikes eating pasta. Yes, it was the Thom Browne corporate staff holiday outing. TB himself was at the head of the table.

Out-of-towners were riveted.

"What's with the Hutterites, or whatever the fuck they are?" asked one well-lubricated diner.

"The Branch Davidians are in the house!" slurred another.

Thom just smiled and ate his pasta.

the olsens vs the phoenix suns

MOST PEOPLE, when they hear the word "Arizona," think about golf carts and spa facials, or Alice Cooper, or horrible sweat lodges gone awry, or extremely tall sports personalities living in potentate splendor in their Sun Valley palazzos. Not me. When I visit Phoenix, I always think about *Psycho*.

The images of Janet Leigh embezzling from her boss and then fleeing into the sticks, only to be hacked to death in the bathroom of a run-down motel by a troubled young man who wears his mum's old frocks because he believes that "a boy's best friend is his mother," were seared into my brain in the sixties and have remained there ever since. When I fly over downtown Phoenix, I try to identify the famous building from the opening scene. Yes, I'm talking about the location of Janet Leigh's clandestine lunchtime shag. Was it that building there?

Fall 2009. The plane is coming in to land at Phoenix Sky Harbor International Airport and, yes, I am thinking about Janet Leigh in her pointy white brassiere, but I am also thinking about the Olsens. One half of them is on the plane with me. Mary-Kate and I are flying in to present a trunk show and *défilé* at Barneys Scottsdale. Ashley arrived a couple of days earlier for a little poolside R & R, and is now hiding under a parasol, one assumes.

Let's talk about the mind-blowing success of the Row. Mary-Kate and Ashley Oslen are the only entertainment celebrities in the history of fashion to have achieved a Carine-Roitfeld-thinks-we're-fabulous high-fashion cred. They even won the CFDA Designer of the Year Award. No other celebrity has accomplished this feat. Madge and Gwen may have made some dough in the tweenie zone, Jessica Simpson may have cha-ching'd at Macy's, but the Olsens are the only *People* mag iconettes to see their clothing hang in stores alongside Lanvin, Dries Van Noten, Comme des Garçons and Alaia. They have achieved *acceptance*.

Their designs are uncompromising. Called the Row in homage to Brit tailoring epicenter Savile Row, their collection is chic, elegant, cerebral, modern and pared down. And expensive. In 2011 they launched a handbag line that included a $39,000 croc backpack. Barneys sold three of them.

The former *Full House* stars and I are staging this fashion show for the delectation of an organization named the Wives of the Phoenix Suns. The event will raise some money for their foundation while simultaneously introducing the basketball wives to a label of which they may have hitherto been unaware.

While Mary-Kate joins Ashley in the Barneys alteration shop for last-minute fittings on their models, I twirl round the store making sure everything looks spiffy.

At six o'clock the twins are ready, and I am all poofy and perfumed and gussied up and ready to meet the basketball wives.

By the way, when I say perfumed, I mean *perfumed*!

I am a big believer in sloshing it on. Yes, I know that's very trashy and parvenu and seventies of me, but I enjoy being trashy and parvenu and seventies. When people complain about headaches and allergies caused by the overfragrancing of others, I just think they have a bad attitude. My fragrance role model is the Sabu character in *Black Narcissus*, the gorgeous Technicolor Michael Powell movie. The bejeweled and turbaned prince rides to the hilltop convent on his little white pony for his daily lessons, reeking of perfume and intoxicating the poor nuns against their will. Go Sabu.

Suddenly, there is a colorful commotion at the front door of Barneys. It appears as if a group of exotic birds is attempting to gain entry. That, as it turns out, is exactly what is happening.

As they approach, I can see that these birds of paradise are carrying purses—colorful, embellished handbags with inlays of fluorescent python and jangling charms. And they are wearing cocktail dresses—exotically pleated, patterned and ruched. With their explosive coiffures and bravura maquillages, the Suns basketball wives resemble gorgeous prize-winning cockatiels. And they smell *delicious*.

Striking alluring attitudes and emitting wafts of Fracas and Frederic Malle, the lusciously beautiful and bejeweled ladies arrange themselves—a collage of pretzeled bare legs and brimming cleavages—in their front-row seats. The Row show begins, and a dramatic and fascinating dissonance reveals itself.

One by one, the models emerge. They are minimalist mavens in simple shapes. Slate gray, charcoal black, and petrol blue are the dominant hues. The designs are austere and graphic.

With their seaweedy hair and pasty pallor, the models appear to be in the middle of some kind of existentialist crisis. They are very Pina Bausch. The garments hang straight from their shoulders, reminding me of Norman Bates when he wears his mother's frocks. Like Norman, the models have no curves.

The basketball wives, in sharp contrast, have lots of curves, but the differences do not end there.

The basketball wives are happy.

The Row models are haunted and melancholy.

The basketball wives are a redolent bouquet.

The Row models smell of soap and water.

The basketball wives look as if they have migrated from Costa Rica.

The Row gals don't fly. They live in an orphanage or an incredibly chic mental hospital.

Never in the history of runway shows has there ever been a wider chasm between the gals *on* the runway and the gals staring *at* the runway.

They are like two different species, a seraglio of exotic odalisques observing a conclave of überchic fashion nuns. Cher meets Mother Teresa. Carmen Miranda goes on a date with Jane Goodall. Exuberance versus earnestness. Flamboyance versus restraint.

Sex versus fashion.

Show a hot-blooded man a photograph of deathly pale Cate Blanchett in an exquisite varicose-vein-colored Givenchy couture creation, and the chances of him puffing up his chest and saying, "I'd like to tap that!" are, let's face it, girls, a tad remote.

When horny hetero hunks observe Tilda Swinton looking

androgynous and otherworldly in a Haider Ackermann jimmy-jammy suit or a Raf Simons canary yellow shroud, it is difficult to imagine them popping a Viagra and saying, "Okay, Tilly! Let's do it!"

If a testosterone-riddled frat boy encountered the hauntingly chic Daphne Guinness lurking in the shadows at the kegger, would he try to slip her a roofie and slip a hand in her blouse . . . or would he run back to his dorm room and begin garlanding his access points with garlic while clutching a crucifix? As filled with admiration for the style of the Right Honorable Daphne as I am, I am going to go with the latter.

What's my point?

My point is that high fashion is simply NOT sexy. High fashion is conceptual and strange and intriguing and startling . . . but *hot?* Not so much.

Leandra Medine, a highly strung, brilliant, style-addicted Manhattaness, has always understood the intrinsic unhotness of La Mode. This is why, when she began writing her fashion blog, she wisely named it the Man Repeller.*

---

* Here is her definition:

man·re·pell·er [mahn-ree-peller]

—noun: outfitting oneself in a sartorially offensive way that will result in repelling members of the opposite sex. This includes but is not limited to harem pants, boyfriend jeans, overalls (see: *human repelling*), shoulder pads, full-length jumpsuits, jewelry that resembles violent weaponry and clogs.

—verb (used without object),**-pell·ing, -pell·ed.**

to commit the act of repelling men:

Girl 1: What are you wearing tonight?

Girl 2: My sweet lime green drop-crotch utility pants.

Girl 1: Oh, so we're man repelling tonight?

Leandra is a smart girl. She recognized that esoteric fashion is, by definition, almost a *denial* of sex. In order to make clothing look and feel like "high fashion," a designer needs to strip away any suggestion of man-pleasing hoochie allure.

Back to the show.

With the exception of the moment when I introduced the ladies as "the wives of the Phoenix Pistons"—I try to stay au courant with sports teams, but there are so bloody many!—the show went off without a hitch.

At the après-show meet 'n' shop, the birds of paradise and the little gray sparrows finally encountered one another in person. They hit it off surprisingly well. Each species scrutinized the feathers and behaviors of its polar opposite and was amused and intrigued. Nobody ate anybody.

The good-natured basketball wives cherry-picked their way through the Row offerings and, paradoxically, found the items which could be integrated into what I imagined were their vast and colorful closets. The indigo python jackets, in particular, were a big hit.

As I observed the gals interacting after the show, I could not help but ask myself the obvious question: If I had been born a chick, would I be a man repeller? Would I dress like a flamboyant bird of paradise or an existentialist fashion missionary? Would I be able to put conceptual fashion esoterica ahead of my need to dazzle and mesmerize and tantalize? Could I turn my back on flashy, frothy sensuality and, instead, take the steep and rugged path to subtlety?

My first impulse would be to lie and say, "Yes, bring me the

Yohji burlap onesie! I will live a life of fashionable aesthetic purity."

Life, however, is short. As much as I love and appreciate the Row and the other designers who inhabit the codified world of nuance and sophistication, I fear I just might be a burlesque bitch at heart. I'll take a Jeff Koons over a Richard Serra any day.

coco was a
jersey girl

HAS YOUR DRY CLEANER ever unpicked and removed the label from your Margiela blouse—those four white signature stitches—and skillfully reattached it so that it could *not* be seen from the outside?

Has your mother ever mended and patched the artfully chewed holes in your ripped-to-pieces Balmain jeans?

Remember the Miyake shroud that came back from the cleaners sans pleats. Did you return it and whimper, "Can I have my pleats back, please? Pleats. Please?"

Did your dad ever offer to remove the massive padlock from your Chloé Paddington bag, using his chain cutter, to prevent said bag from pulling your arm out of its socket?

Sometimes people, non–fashion people, *they just don't get it.*

The ideas and concepts which are brewed and concocted in the rarefied cloisters of the fashion asylum, sometimes, once they encounter the cold, objective light of the outside world, suddenly change in meaning, or have no meaning, or even take on an utterly unintentional meaning.

A couple of decades ago, I once walked across lower Manhattan wearing a nifty knee-length black jacket. I was rocking a new-wave undertaker look. I had purchased this garment from some tailor in the UK who specialized in teddy-boy clothing. Back in the day, it was called a "drape coat."

Everything started off great. No problems in the West Village. In SoHo everyone thought I looked groovy. Then I headed to the northeast. I was visiting a pal who lived near Tompkins Square Park. 'Ere long I reached the Bowery. This is back before there was a Whole Foods and a happening Bowery Hotel. These streets resembled the set of *The Omega Man* minus Charlton Heston.

"Back to your own neighborhood, Yentl!" yelled some guy who was warming himself in front of an improvised brazier. Yes, this drug-addled street warrior had mistaken me for a Hasid. *Oy veh*.

I sincerely hope that when this kind of thing happens, you are able to maintain your sangfroid. As you clutch your formerly pleated Miyake, it is important to see the bigger picture. Keep in mind that fashion is an insular, codified place, which speaks in a language of its own. The cues are hard to read. Even I, *moi*, occasionally draw the wrong fashion conclusions.

Despite having inhabited the fashion asylum for such a long time, I am still capable of misreading the signals. Like Nomi Malone, Elizabeth Berkley's character in the movie *Showgirls*, I am still capable of turning "Versahchie" into "Versayce."

It was just a typical Tuesday evening. I am sure the same scenario was unfolding in households all over the United States. My husband was watching *Lockup*, the grim MSNBC documentary series about life inside our roughest prisons. I was sprawled on the carpet next to Liberace, our aging Norwich terrier. While I flipped lazily through the month's *Vogue* magazine, Liberace snored. Just a normal American family vignette.

Suddenly, I stopped flipping. Something shocking caught my eye. A new perfume from the house of Chanel titled . . . drumroll . . . *Jersey*. The editorial described it as "relaxed chic with a dash of liberation."

I was intrigued. Very intrigued.

A fragrant homage to our Garden State, created by the legendary French fashion house?

Did not see that coming.

Whatever had possessed the folks at Maison Chanel to draw a dotted line—nay, a veritable Jersey Turnpike—from the refined luxury of the Rue Cambon to the gritty realities of New Jersey, America's eleventh most populous state?

Coco Chanel led a complex and unconventional life. A prewar romantic sojourn in Atlantic City would not have been out of the question. Maybe one year she just said, "Fuck it! I'm so over this whole Riviera situation!" and boated across the Atlantic to New Jersey. And there was an even stronger connection: let's not forget the fact that Mademoiselle Chanel invented something that eventually became synonymous with the Jersey Shore. The suntan.

Once upon a time, tans were exclusively associated with rowdy peasants. The likelihood of running into Madame de Pompadour or Queen Victoria at Fay's Rays or Dazzle Me

Bronze (these are the names of actual contemporary tanning salons) was a big fat zero. Fashionable aristocratic women were so terrified of looking rugged and outdoorsy that they would put all kinds of demented stuff on their faces: we're talking rice powder and white powdered lead. I am not exactly sure what white powdered lead is, but chances are those lead-loving ladies did not survive many summers.

Then, in the 1920s, trendsetter Chanel went on a boat trip and forgot to bring her sunbonnet. Coco got baked. She returned to shore looking daringly dusky. Mademoiselle's *nouvelle couleur* caused a sensation in Deauville, the Jersey Shore of the French haute bourgeoisie. Before long, every courtesan and countess in every cabana from Copacabana to Coney Island was sporting a healthy agrarian glow. All thanks to Coco.

Over the subsequent decades, tans became associated with an emerging groovy jet set—the starlets, playboys, and effete aristos. Pale people worked in factories while tanned beautiful people zipped off to Ibiza and Saint Tropez. Eventually the pale proletariat—including my mum, Betty Doonan, in the sixties—figured it out. Mum did not get to spend July lolling on a yacht with Liz Taylor in Acapulco, but there was no reason why she should not look as if she had. All Mater had to do was plug in that scary, crackly-sounding sunlamp while watching the telly after a hard day at the plant.

Back to that family vignette and that fragrance named "Jersey."

"Could it be," I mused as I read my *Vogue*, "that the folks at Chanel HQ have just decided, surprisingly and shockingly, to capitalize on the popularity of the *Jersey Shore* reality television show." Could the powerful reverse chic of J Woww, the Situation et al have proven too irresistible?

Having just, that very day, walked the block from the Barneys midtown office to catch the Barnes & Noble signing for Snooki's new book, *Confessions of a Guidette*, I understood the fascination. Jersey was having an undeniable moment. Jersey was on a roll. Jersey was *le dernier cri*.

Clarification came only after I dug into the *Vogue* editorial. According to the writer, Jersey does indeed occupy a very special place in the Chanel legend. But we are talking fabric here, not guidos. One of Coco Chanel's great innovations was to take cotton knit jersey, a fabric previously only utilized for men's undergarments, and use it to create thoroughly modern sportif separates for early-twentieth-century women, thereby relieving them of the bondage of Belle Époque corsetry. The new Jersey perfume pays homage to this revolutionary moment in fashion history.

Frankly, I am a little concerned that the marketing folks at Chanel may have overestimated our ability to recalibrate our response to the word "Jersey." The Garden State, after all, has long since occupied a very significant spot in the American psyche. Dip into the history and culture of New Jersey and you will see exactly what I am talking about. A staggering number of iconic and influential Americans hail from this frequently mocked state: Lesley Gore, Dorothy Parker, Rachel Zoe, Connie Francis, Debbie Harry, Patti Smith and a rather fabulous pipe-smoking fashion-editor-turned-politico named Millicent Fenwick.

Inspired by the *Vogue* piece, I sallied forth to purchase a bottle of Jersey from the Chanel store in SoHo. I intended to buy it as a gift for Chelsea Handler, a New Jersey native and the queen of late-night TV.

I envisaged Miss Handler—she frequently riffs on her tawdry-but-fabulous home state—having some good old-fashioned fun cross-referencing the top notes of musk and lavender with the *Jersey Shore* gang and the table-flipping *Real Housewives* of said state.

"Jersey is sold out!" declared the helpful sales associate.

Clearly the multiple resonances of the word "Jersey" were working their magic. I called a couple of other stores and got the same response. Locating a bottle of Jersey was harder than squeezing Governor Chris Christie into an Ed Hardy tube top. Bam!

The launch of Chanel's Jersey called to mind another lost-in-translation fragrance debacle. About five years ago, Balenciaga launched a new perfume. The folks at Maison Balenciaga became perplexed when this new product received a less than enthusiastic reception in the United States. With their designer, Nicolas Ghesquière, hitting his stride—every chick on earth was carrying one of those bags with the dangly bits—they felt sure that the perfume would be an automatic hit.

The name?

"Poupée."

Unaware that *poupée* (pronounced "poo-pay") was the French word for "doll," American consumers saw only a perverse and horrible attempt to combine the aromas of poop and pee, and felt compelled to ask themselves, "Just how sick are these sordid Frogs?"

Bottom line: The Balenciaga folks had overestimated the linguistic capabilities of us Yanks. (I became a citizen in 2009.) Barneys New York was the one U.S. store that dared to retail the provocatively named fragrance. Many customers purchased it as a gag gift: "Here! I know you like rare and exotic fragrances. Have some poopee!"

Back to Jersey.

My TV-addicted husband proudly hails from the southern Jersey town of Bridgeton. He frequently waxes rhapsodic about his fellow Jerseyites, a lack of pretension being the most frequently highlighted trait. Jonny claims that it is virtually impossible to put on airs if you are from New Jersey. As a result, straight-talkin' Jerseyans are in many ways the polar opposite of, say, French people.

If you are from New Jersey, you could never, as Coco Chanel did, go around saying absurd things like "Elegance is refusal" or making haughty statements like "Luxury lies . . . in the absence of vulgarity. *Vulgarity* is the ugliest word in our language. I stay in the game to fight it."

If you were born in New Jersey, you need not waste your life tilting against the windmills of vulgarity. Instead you can embrace it with a shriek of delight and an oily, suntanned embrace.

the cellulite closet

ONE SWEATY SUMMER EVENING not too long ago, I attended a lecture at New York University titled "Fat Porn." A combination of curiosity seekers, chubby chasers and fresh-faced students packed the lecture hall. The anticipation was palpable. You could have heard a pin drop.

The talk was delivered by a lady who described herself as a BBW, a big beautiful woman. A three-hundred-pounder, this broad was a proud and evangelical member of the online community of fat-porn entrepreneurs who tantalize vast numbers of fat fetishizers on a daily basis.

I am not sure what the point of her lecture was, or why parents pay good money to send their kids to fancy colleges to hear this kind of stuff, but I can tell you this much: It was a riveting and unforgettable experience.

The slide show was undoubtedly my favorite part of the evening. Each genre of fat porn—there are many and they are shockingly specific—was illustrated with disarmingly explicit photography. For example: The fat-fetish category known as "Not Fitting" was accompanied by a shot of a huge lingerie-clad chick who was stuck—physically, irrevocably, massively—in the doorway of a hotel room. Her face was a magical combo of lascivious delight and discomfort. According to our BBW lecturess, there are large groups of men who find the notion of not fitting, as vividly depicted in this image, to be the apex of erotic fantasia. To my eyes, it seemed more like a scene from an old episode of *The Benny Hill Show*, or *The Honeymoon Killers* starring Shirley Stoler, or a still from a John Waters movie starring Edith Massey, or all of the above.

There was also a category called "Squashing." The accompanying photograph showed a middle-aged businessman wearing thick black spectacles à la Martin Scorsese, lying on a bed, fully clothed and still clutching his briefcase. No duvet for him! In lieu of bedding, he was covered by a scantily clad BBW of gargantuan proportions. She was gleefully squishing the life out of him. The squashee was gleeful too.

There were other categories, like "Messy Eating" and "Growing." I won't elaborate upon those in particular, but will let your imaginations fill in the blanks. Besides, we need to get to more pressing stuff. We need to address the plus-size, garter-belt-wearing elephant in the room: What the hell was I doing at this lecture?

I feel confident that the answer to this question will surprise you. Here goes.

I am fascinated by fat. Having worked in the fat-fascistic

world of style for forty years, I am always struggling to shine a light on the fatorexic paradoxes and fat-phobic blind spots which haunt the fashion universe. My goal is to pry open the cellulite closet and let the sunshine in.

My profound interest in the psychology of large women and in plus-size clothing has taken me places where a 140-pound dude ought not to go. I have attended sordid and terrifying lectures at NYU, and I have seen things a bloke ought not to see. I have prowled the "hefty hideaways" of Manhattan. I have seen muumuus the size of circus tents, and I've seen halter tops the size of . . .

The mid 2000s.

My friend Anne had recently become the designer for legend-ary plus-size mega–chain store Lane Bryant. She scored me a front-row seat at the showing of her first LB collection, where I found myself next to one of my all-time favorite style icons, Mr. Isaac Hayes. Yes, I'm talking about Mr. Shaft, Mr. Hot Buttered Soul, Mr. Chef from *South Park*.

On this occasion, Mr. Hayes was wearing a vivid metallic-orange-lamé-embellished caftan with matching pants. He had the air of a visiting dignitary. As the show unfurled, Isaac be-came quite vocal. Every time a new plus-size diva sallied forth, he would purr and growl appreciatively into my ear.

"These young ladies are . . . deliciously endowed . . . deeeliciously endowed . . . deliciously endooowed!"

Anne was excited about her first collection and wanted to show me the new season's deliveries in situ. At the time, there was only one Lane Bryant store in Manhattan. It was in Harlem.

A schlep, but Anne assured me it would be worth it. She lured me onto the A train with the following exotic promise: "I bet you've never fondled a criss-cross halter top in a size twenty-eight before, have you?"

I had not.

Before you could say "badonka-donk-donk," or even plain old "badonk," we were winging our way north. Upon arrival, Anne dragged me through the front door of the store and straight to a very focused offering of leopard-print merchandise. Yes, leopard print. We're talking pants, shirts, even a baby-doll party dress with an underwire bra built in. The message was clear: Just because you are gigantic, it does not mean that you have to hide your light under a beige bushel. Au contraire! Swathe yourself in predatory, glamorous animal print and get massively feline on their asses. The only thing small about these saucy, hedonistic garments was the price tag; a kicky leopard slip dress with lace-up sides was twenty-five dollars. Wildly affordable clothing for the deliciously endowed.

There is something profoundly joyful and supersassy about the whole idea of large confident ladies bouncing around in leopard separates. Plus-size clothing is often so dismal and self-effacing, the ugly stepsister of her anorexic high-fashion sister. Not here.

I told Anne that if I had been mayor of Harlem, I would have mandated the wearing of leopard. Any large chick not rocking a leopard *quelque chose* would be forced to explain herself. My enthusiasm for the leopard offerings caught the attention of the manager, who guided me over to a rack of what looked like beach hammocks on hangers. As I examined the draped and gathered yards of white canvas, I saw myself swinging back and forth between a couple of palm trees and enjoying a Tommy Bahama Margaritaville moment.

"Voilà!" interjected Anne. "Up to size twenty-eight. A great seller."

These were the legendary criss-cross boulder holders which had lured me on this expedition. Magnificently huge, they came in a dizzying range of colors, fabrications and permutations: acid-green fake-croc ciré, crisp nautical navy and white cotton, luxe maroon Ultrasuede, etc. My favorite was definitely the fake-croc ciré.

While I came to terms with the total lack of hanger appeal in these immense garments, Anne elaborated upon the upsides of a plus-size halter: "If a big chick wears a muumuu, she invariably looks like a mountain. A halter top, on the other hand, actually bisects and minimizes her upper torso, and it shows off her arms . . . and we plumper girls have gorgeous arms."

On cue, a zaftig young shopper runwayed out of the fitting room in a white halter looking deliciously endowed and gorgeously empowered. She received a well-deserved ripple of applause. Her arms did indeed appear succulent and appealing.

What about the bottoms?

Anne tossed me a pair of fifty-dollar snakeskin-print jeans—this plus-size missile nearly knocked me over, such was the weight and volume of fabric—and a forty-dollar Capri pant in black stretch cotton.

(Yes, Capri pant, singular. We fashion asylum inhabitants reserve the right to randomly singularize and pluralize. In this regard, there are no rules. Sometimes it's a "jean" and sometimes it's a "pair of jeans." It might be a "pair of Manolos," but it could just as easily be a "Manolo." As in: "I'm rocking my new Celine tunic with a hoop [earring] and a Manolo." Wearing a "Manolo" in no way suggests that an amputation has occurred.)

While more bodacious, deliciously endowed shoppers poured in through the front door, Anne spewed plus-size wisdom for the benefit of anyone within earshot.

"Narrow the upper torso, girls, and draw attention to everything below the knee with strappy shoes and a damn good pedicure."

I glanced at Anne's toes. They glowed with vermillion perfection.

"If you are procrastinating about purchasing a particular garment," continued Anne, "then visualize it in a size six, and then ask yourself, 'Would a skinny fashion addict like Madonna or Kate go bat-shit over this item?' If the answer is no, then close your handbag."

Buzzing with the clarity of Anne's advice, we bid farewell to the staff and customers and staggered out into the broiling heat of 125th Street.

The sidewalk was packed with proud, chunky African-American goddesses of all ages, strutting their stuff and basking in the admiring gazes and compliments of every man on the street. Needless to say, the playful and nondiscriminatory badinage was invariably directed at the ladies with magnificently pronounced derrières.

As we rattled back downtown on the A train, I reflected upon the key points of Anne's fat-fashion lecture. One thing seemed clear: If you are a larger lady, then maybe you should move to Harlem or at the very least shop there. African-American chicks never seem to let a few excess pounds come between them and their desire for some fashion flamboyance. The same cannot be said of "whitey."

February 2007, Fashion Week.

Victoria Beckham shocks the fashion monde by announcing that she will be eschewing size-zero gals in favor of one Daniella Sarahyba. The 35-26-36 Brazilian would, according to VB, represent the image of her upcoming collection.

Was this a visionary flesh-positive gesture or one of calculated cunning?

The always charitable British tabloids wasted no time in accusing Mrs. Beckham—they have referred to her as "Skeletal Spice" for years—of opting for larger gals in order to make herself look thin when she trots out to take her catwalk bows. You know, *that* age-old trick.

Whatever the reason, Mrs. Beckham reignited a frenzied debate about fat.

This is by no means the first time this has happened, and it certainly won't be the last. Every so often fashion has a pang of fat guilt. Once in a while somebody shines a revealing light, as La Beckham did, on the chasm between the thinness of the runway models and the fleshy abundance of real women, and fashion, God bless her little cotton socks, is forced to respond.

On these occasions, fashion goes into spin mode.

Fashion starts by very publicly castigating herself for always depicting/hiring/photographing such thin girls. Naughty fashion!

Fashion then promises to mend her ways.

Fashion vows to use bigger girls.

Fashion insists that she will henceforth check the body-mass index of those for-god's-sake-give-that-skinny-bitch-a-ham-sandwich models.

And so it was on this occasion . . .

Statements were issued. Commitments were made. A debate about thinness started to rage and threatened to turn this particular Fashion Week into a veritable fat summit. This was a good thing: it gave us fashion folk an issue, something really meaty, upon which to chew while waiting for those three-hundred-plus shows to begin.

For a fat researcher of long standing, this moment presented a sizzling opportunity. I lost no time in soliciting opinions about the Beckham-instigated fat fracas.

"I thought models were supposed to be skinny," said a remarkably svelte Carson Kressley, when I cornered him before the John Bartlett show and asked his opinion about the latest eruptions of anorexia/fashion hysteria. He was wearing a formfitting primrose cardigan and skinny jeans tucked into riding boots.

"I myself live on a steady diet of Ex-Lax and grapefruit juice," hissed the lovable Carson, as the first model came striding down the runway.

After the show, I headed backstage in the hopes of checking the body-mass index of the skinnier models. I also wanted to see if Mr. Bartlett had followed the CFDA's newly issued bulimia-battling guidelines, in particular the one suggesting that designers "supply healthy meals, snacks and water backstage and at shoots, and provide nutrition and fitness education."

After scouring the backstage area for snacks and seminars— and finding none—I congratulated the beefy Mr. Bartlett on a great show and asked him for the male perspective. His response was chilling.

"I'm surrounded by girls, gorgeous models, and they all think they are fat. Guys don't get crazy about that stuff."

Hmm. If girls are somehow predisposed to succumb to self-punitive eating disorders, maybe it really is time for intervention at a higher level? Maybe Congress should follow the example of the Spanish authorities and start calibrating limbs and counting calories for girls at risk.

"The government has bigger fish to fry. Pardon the expression," opined Mr. Kressley.

Sunday afternoon: The DVF show.

Diane von Furstenberg knows a thing or two about fat. Her wrap dresses perform a specific lard-retaining function, to a point. If you are fat, the wrap will not make you thin. But if you are normal, i.e., you have those wobbly bits around your middle because you deem it necessary to ingest the occasional meal, a wrap dress will sharpen up your silhouette.

As we waited for the show to start, a fevered seminar raged as the fashion insiders divulged what they had eaten so far that day. (It was but four o'clock.) Some interesting patterns emerged. British fashionistas seemed to have a less neurotic relationship to food than their American counterparts. *Harper's Bazaar* editor in chief Glenda Bailey, who had already eaten a poached egg on toast and a bowl of soup, revealed all, in her signature North English lilt.

"Ooh, luv! At *Harper's Bazaar*, we looove food as much as we looove fashion."

Fellow Brit and *Marie Claire* editor in chief Joanna Coles— she has just gone to *Cosmo* at the time of writing—proudly declared that she had just eaten a bowl of mashed potatoes "with lashings of butter."

Of all the women I spoke to, supermodel-turned-commentator Veronica Webb had eaten the most. "Chicken satay, french fries, yogurt and this amazing stuff called Bagel French Toast." This confirmed my suspicion that African-American fashionistas enjoy a more easygoing relationship with food than their Caucasian co-citizens.

Robin Givhan of *The Washington Post* weighed in on this issue: "We black women aren't so hung up about food," declared the Pulitzer Prize winner, adding, "That's why I happily ate a bowl of pasta this morning. But the fashion person in me did not allow me to eat the bread which came with it."

The show began, finally, with an intriguing black-taffeta version of the signature wrap, worn by a gal who definitely looked as if she could use a cheeseburger or seven.

So where were all the plumper gals?

They were hauntingly absent.

As the late great Franco Moschino once said, "Fashion is full of CHIC!"

Sunday five p.m.: It was so bloody cold that I bagged any further shows and ran home to catch Super Bowl XLI. After staring at all those haunted, wraithlike models, the adorable

Indianapolis cheerleaders were a real picker-upper. With their 1950s physiques, these doll-like cuties possessed an optimistic joie de vivre not shared by those poor stringy melancholics in the Bryant Park tents.

As I watched the Colts–Bears game, I thought of all the blokes across the country boozing, belching, farting and munching their way through the Super Bowl. How different from the perverse fashion front row. Unlike sports, fashion is not about bracing fresh air and blood-pumping physicality.

Fashion is perverse. Fashion, foncy elitist designer fashion, has always, and will always be, an arch, sick, twisted bitch. High fashion has never been a cozy, caring sister. She has always been a tortured, idealized freak.

Elizabethan women wore corsets with wooden slats.

Victorian women dilated their pupils—they wanted their eyes to appear sparkling and engaging—with drops of belladonna (deadly nightshade).

Chinese style addicts bound their feet into rotting, misshapen little hooves.

Turkish women wore neck corsets!

Looking for healthy role models in the world of fashion, or trying to legislate them, is a total waste of time. This situation will never change, because fashion is not in the business of selling the bouncy, the smiley, the feel-good, the inclusive and the kumbaya, my Lord.

Fashion is about selling the esoteric, the fantastical and the wickedly fabulous.

Every once in a while, dame fashion will have one of those guilt spasms and go through the motions of pretending she's strawberry shortcake. And then, just when you're getting comfy, she'll do a total volte-face. She will slam her town-car door shut, drive off peeling rubber and become more fabulously freaky, more unhealthy and more gloriously demented than ever.

Where does that leave the plus-sizer?

I sympathize with the bouncy broads of the world. I feel the pain of the chunky chicks. You gals are tantalized and mesmerized by the mirage of fashion, but if you dare to go shopping with the intention of purchasing nice-ies and ice-ies for yourself, you face certain disappointment and rejection. (As a dinky male, I have faced the same marginalization.) The world of designer fashion is unwelcoming to you. My stylish-but-zaftig girlfriends voice their complaints to me all the time.

"Plus-size stores are a waistless land, a ghetto of boxy clothes in horrid prints and cheap fabrics."

"You come out of the fitting room looking like you're wearing a pup tent."

"Last week some shop assistant in Zara asked me if I was the star of the movie *Precious*."

Starved of designer fashion, my pals satiate their fashion cravings with oversexed stilettos, jeweled Pashminas, huge tribal necklaces and outré purses and bags.

It's a measure of the stupidity-bordering-on-retardation of many people who are working in the fashion industry that they remain oblivious to the opportunity represented by the growing, and I do mean growing, number of fashion-starved broads who are size twelve and rising. This situation represents a massive opportunity. To paraphrase Samantha Foxx: Bigger broads need designer clothes too.

So fashion, listen up! I'm talking to you.

You can stay in your twisted, sick, codified, freaky zone of creativity. We need you to stay there in order to generate insane and provocative new ideas. And you can use all the skinny skeletons you want. Just do me one favor: Please make designer drag in bigger sizes. (And smaller sizes for men!) That's all I ask.

manischewitz?
j'adore!

RECENTLY A FRIEND OF MINE, a successful luxury retail exec, was bitching about his demanding and highly strung clientele.

"These are my people, but they are such a bunch of annoying JAPs."

I asked him about his WASP clients: "Aren't they just as quixotic and high maintenance?"

"I wouldn't know. I never had any."

Though clearly indulging in a little playful exaggeration, he was nonetheless making a point. Jews are synonymous with fashion. Jews are the glamorous gasoline which has powered the fashion industry through the last century. Whether flogging *schmattas* or buying them, they are integral to the vitality and well-being of La Mode.

I thought about my Jews a lot during the whole Galliano debacle.

John Galliano, for those of you who just flew in from Mars,

was the fashion designer—nay, the brilliant magician—at the illustrious house of Christian Dior, convicted of making anti-Semitic comments during a drunken rant in a Paris bar.

It was a horrible implosion, like something out of a Zola novel. The mighty creative impresario, the bloke who would take his deserved curtain calls with such stylish and often hilarious panache, reduced to a ranting mess in the corner of a bar. Watching the video, I was reminded of Gervaise, the booze-addicted, downward-spiraling heroine of *L'Assommoir*, and also of some of my Irish relatives, namely my uncle Dave and, yes, my Belfast grandpa.

Of all the oaths and notions that could have popped out of Mr. Galliano's mouth when he was out of his skull, it struck me as strange and illogical that it should have been that Jew stuff. Why not rant about the unfairness of the British class system or the snooty superiority of the French? Or the annoying, eavesdropping concierge in his Paris apartment building? Why the Jews?

Did John believe the stuff he was saying? I am sure he did not. It was the drink talking. Nonetheless, in the aftermath of *l'affaire Galliano* I found myself thinking a lot about how much I love my Jews. Yes, I married a lovely and talented one too, but there's more to it than that. Much more.

Jews have been good to me. Jews helped me find refuge in the fashion asylum. Jews paid me to do stuff when I was barely qualified to do *anything*. Jews have always put a roof over my head. They helped me back when I was young, feral, unwashed and ridiculous. I am what you might call a major, lifelong mitzvah recipient. There is not enough space here to kvell about all the fabulous Jews who recklessly and generously enabled my she-nanigans over the years, but here are some edited highlights.

In the mid-seventies I dressed windows for a glamorous Jewish couple called Shelley and Tony who had a chain of fashion shops dotted about the London area. These kicky, affordable stores were named—wait for it!—Sheltone Fashions. I would travel from store to store, changing the merch in the windows and szhooshing up the store interiors.

Being young and stupid, I decided one fine day to give myself a raise. Without telling either Shelley or Tony, I increased my hourly rate and without further ado sent in my weekly invoice.

Instead of stapling my scrotum to the nearest telegraph pole, Mr. Tony called me and very sweetly explained that any raises would need to be negotiated and that they were not something which one could simply award oneself.

While working for Shelley and Tony, I picked up extra clams moonlighting at a Jewish-owned office-lady fashion boutique in the City of London named City Girl Jennifer. I never met Jennifer. But I did meet a cast of hilarious Jewish salesladies who taught me the meaning of many strange words, including "yenta," "mieskeit," "verputz," "shonda," "sheitel," "shykel" and "meshuga." These high-street jobs gave me an extensive knowledge of Yiddish and a wealth of display experience.

In the late seventies I was plucked from this chiaro-obscurity by a brilliant, creative, eccentric Jew named Tommy Perse, who sponsored my green card and gave me a job at his store, Maxfield, an iconic temple of chic in West Hollywood.

To say he took a leap of faith is no exaggeration. Back then I was wilder, younger and even more disaster prone. I relied heavily on my Jewish safety net, and Tommy always came through. When the engine fell out of my '65 Dodge push-button station wagon, Tommy good-naturedly coughed up the dough for repairs. When I got busted for drunk driving while wearing a plaid bondage punk outfit, Tommy helped me find a lawyer.

I would still be working at Maxfield if the equally creative and brilliant Gene Pressman had not given me my job at Barneys, where I have schlepped happily for more than twenty-five years.

My transition into a writing career has also been Jew-inspired. In 1998, Peter Kaplan, now at Fairchild and formerly of *The New York Observer*, read my first book, a book I assumed would be a one-off writing venture, and bravely offered me the opportunity to write a regular column. Ten years later, courtesy of Jacob Weisberg, I skipped onto Slate.com. The book you are holding in your hands would not exist without the vision and chutzpah of publishing-world Jew David Rosenthal and demi-Jewess Sarah Hochman. Mazel tov to moi!

Why did my Jews feel compelled to extend a helping hand to this flailing *feygele?* Maybe it is because they too are members of a marginalized and oft-reviled group. The difference between a pink triangle and a yellow star is, after all, only a color switch and three more points. Which very much brings us back to the fragile, talented Mr. Galliano.

I suspect that John Galliano could tell a very similar story to mine. How many untold numbers of Jews have supported him over the years? How much of his success does he owe to the kindness and support of Jewish mitzvahs, *machers, schmatta* kings, fashionistas and, most important, customers. News flash: WASPs don't shop! Without the passionate and genuine support of style-obsessed Jewesses, Galliano would probably have ended up stitching frocks for City Girl Jennifer.

I earnestly hope for a positive outcome for John and feel very optimistic about his impending reinvention. In my experience, Jews are magnanimous by nature and will give him the thumbs-up.

Regarding Jewish magnanimity: Back in the nineties I attended the infamous Jean Paul Gaultier fall/winter Jew-inspired runway show. Incorporating bejeweled yarmulkes; oversize, fur-trimmed Hasid hats; and prayer shawls, Jean Paul put his cheeky postmodern spin on every stylish flourish of Orthodox Jewry. Christy Turlington rocked the runway sporting silky payos, and rabbi chic was born. One strapping young model wore a fun-fur Hasid outfit, accessorized with a matching fur-covered ghetto blaster which played "Hava Nagila." This JPG pastiche was strangely beautiful but unquestionably outrageous.

As Jean Paul took his curtain calls, there were a few audible tut-tuts of disapproval.

"I'm offended by that," said the Jew on my left.

"No, you're not," laughed the Jew on my right.

"Okay. You're right. It was great," guffawed the first Jew.

At the time of writing, fashion luminaries are speculating about the status of John's career. According to Cathy Horyn of *The New York Times*, "Some in the fashion industry are wondering if it isn't time to forgive the self-described drug addict and 'lost soul' and offer him a second chance to return to the fashion fold."

Does John need the forgiveness, or otherwise, of the fashion world? In my opinion, he needs something much more beautiful:

he needs sobriety. Rumor has it that he has achieved it. With sobriety will come clarity and a new creative chapter.

Call me crazy, but I see him attending a nice synagogue on Yom Kippur, the holiday of atonement, and explaining in his own words how he fell into the abyss. Jews need to hear it from the man himself. They need to hear that the things he said were part and parcel of an addiction, a madness, an illness from which he has now fully recovered. I think they will listen to him. John is a poet, an artist, a bloke with a sweeping vision, and Jews like that.

plato ripped
my blouse

"SHE IS A LITTLE TOO FAT, but she has a beautiful face and a divine voice." Thus spake Karl Lagerfeld when some journalist or other asked him for his opinion of Adele.

Karl's now legendary quote set the blogosphere afire. The response was explosive and immediate. How dare he? Why is he hating on her? Why is he drinking haterade? Just how full of bile is his daily glass of Châteauneuf-du-Hate?

Karl-gate-hate was major. That relatively innocuous comment, enrobed in praise for Adele's beauty and her voice, was treated as high treason. If he had pulled out a revolver and shot her, he would have received a less outraged response.

I cannot help feeling that the Adele brouhaha would never have gotten any momentum if those young bloggy folks had been more familiar with Karl's gloriously bitchy history. Compared to the other things Karl has said about people over the years, this comment about Adele was so straightforward and so wildly vanilla as to be almost albino. In many ways, Adele got off very lightly.

Karl Lagerfeld is an enduring genius and a true fashion icon. He is also a tart-tongued Teutonic legend of long standing, a guy who is so bitchy that he can be bitchy in six languages, no less. He is the sultan of sarcasm.

When the legendary Pierre Cardin banned the press from his shows later in his career, Karl said, "That's like a woman without lovers asking for the Pill."

When the Metropolitan Museum of Art announced its Jackie Kennedy exhibit, circa 2001, Karl said, "It's perfect. They can call it the Necropolitan Museum." (Karl had hoped that they would mount a Chanel exhibit instead.)

On defeating the deposed president of Chanel: "The good news is that Kitty D'Alessio has been made director of special projects. The bad news is, there are no special projects." (For the record: The glamorous Kitty is a fashion legend—with a serious jet-black side-flip coiffure—who I admire greatly. Her many accomplishments include having masterminded those famous mid-century Maidenform pointy brassiere ads: "I dreamed I went on safari in my Maidenform bra." In *Mad Men* terms, she was the original Peggy.)

On being succeeded at Chloé by Stella McCartney, Karl said, "I think they should have taken a big name. They did—but in music, not fashion."

According to Karl, Miuccia Prada makes "flea-market clothes." And Michael Kors? Lagerfeld told CNN that he had nothing against the American designer, but that was only because he barely knew who he was.

Regarding the adulation surrounding Alaïa: "If you want to see a retrospective of Azzedine Alaïa, just take a look at what he's doing now."

It is important to note that Karl's fabulously reckless bitchiness is often directed toward himself: "I respect nothing, no one, including myself. Respect is not a very creative thing."

And before anyone can make fun of him, he often makes fun of himself.

"When I was four, I asked my mother for a valet for my birthday."

His favorite names? "Louis XIV, Louis XV, Louis XVI."

Who are the Lagerfelds of today? Do they exist? Has this glorious genre of sarcasm gone out of fashion?

I am rather afraid it has. Karl is something of a unicorn. There is a dearth of barbed bon mots. There are no Oscar Wildes or Dorothy Parkers of the runway. Fashion editorials and reviews are always positive. Witty Lagerfeldian denunciations are rare. If you want to enjoy some modish bitchery, you have to trawl back through history in search of these hard-to-find nuggets. Here's a typical example of what I'm talking about: Years ago a pal of mine named Adrian Cartmell launched a collection he dubbed "throw-away chic." The temptation to riff on this concept was too great for one journalist, who opined that "some of it was chic, but most of it should be thrown away."

Forty years later such gems are virtually unheard of.

But please don't despair. There is hope. There exists one brave individual, other than Karl, who is doing all he can to keep it alive.

Not long ago at a fashion cocktail party . . .

An old pal was bending my ear with descriptions of some new low-brow reality-show obsession. (Is there anything more boring than somebody banging on in endless detail about a TV show which one has yet to see?) One particular character had caught his attention. When he described her as "a blousy, braying, tackily dressed plastic surgery victim," I simply could not resist. "For you that must be like looking into a mirror," I said, with a concerned look.

The TV enthusiast winced visibly and strode off. He was later heard telling pals that I was behaving "like a menopausal maniac." When I heard this, I felt a chill wind. Clearly, sarcasm, one of the greatest achievements of mankind, or "unkind" as I prefer to call it, is no longer à la mode.

Sarcasm—the word is from the Greek *sarkazein*, meaning "to rend the flesh"—is one of the building blocks of civilization. The ability to express an unwelcome observation in a wickedly passive-aggressive manner is, at the very least, a great alternative to old-fashioned fisticuffs or rape 'n' pillage. When I think about those ancient Greeks and the carte blanche they enjoyed to say horrid things to each other, I get quite jealous. For example: If you were strolling through downtown Thebes and you ran into a pal who was looking particularly soiled and unkempt, you might say, "Going somewhere special?" to which the other Greek might good-naturedly reply, "Oh, you and your flesh-rending ironic observations!" It's sad to think that such a remark would, in our squishy and oversensitive age, be met with accusations of "hating."

If sarcasm is no longer understood and accepted, then what, pray, will become of the little children of today. Sardonic irony is as critical to healthy child development as vitamins and checking for ticks. Raising your brats on an exclusive diet of sincerity is a recipe for disaster. The current mania for relentless positivity and self-esteem building leaves me convinced that we are in real danger of turning out an entire generation of inspirational speakers. Tony Robbins, watch your back.

Not long ago at another cocktail party . . .

There I was, swanning about at the mingle fest which precedes the Council of Fashion Designers of America Awards at the New York Public Library. This event is not as raucous and freewheeling as you might imagine. When Fashion, with a capital F, celebrates herself, she can get a little serious. The attendees in gowns and tuxes were a tad tight-assed. Adding to the solemnity was the sad fact that Yves Saint Laurent had died the day before. Yves was the quintessence of bohemian, faux-hemian, caftan-wearing Euro-fabulosity. I have a pair of tasseled YSL couture thigh boots which I keep on my mantelpiece as a reminder of this fact.

I was scheduled to present an award to Dries van Noten. Feeling it incumbent on myself to wear Dries, I had ransacked the city for something apropos and found a nifty black kimono thingy. I convinced myself that this jacket, worn with a ruffled white shirt and a narrow tie, fell under that category of "creative black-tie." It screamed jujitsu. I had justified it to myself as "something David Beckham might wear." When I arrived, a pal commented on my ensemble.

"You look as if you bolted out of the salon chair prematurely in that black tent they make you wear. I half expected to see chunks of foil in your hair."

So far, so good.

Then I ran into Dries van Noten himself and drew his attention to my purchase. He seemed to have no recollection of ever designing it. "You look very *Kill Bill*," he said.

Glowing from all this positive attention, I went to grab a drink. The barman seemed happy to see me.

"How is the show going? Do you think you will get another season?"

"Which of my blockbuster media appearances are you referring to?"

"You're on *Will & Grace*, right? Aren't you Beverley Leslie?"

Before I had time to decide if this constituted an insult, a gonging sound drowned out further conversation, indicating that we should take our places for the awards ceremony.

Hostess Fran Lebowitz was *très drôle*. Nonetheless, even she was having a hard time injecting the mood with levity. The crowd felt stiff and self-conscious. An enema was required. At the very least, a laxative. Somebody needed to loosen everyone up. Would Yves have wanted us to be glum all evening? *Pas du tout!* Somebody should really take it upon him or herself to inject these proceedings with a little raucous informality.

Then it occurred to me: Maybe that someone should be *moi*!

I headed for the podium to present Monsieur van Noten, the most talented designer present, with his "International" award. Overcome with feelings of altruism and responsibility, I vowed to use my brief stage appearance to perk up the crowd. A little British debunkery. That's all that is ever needed.

Fran introduces me. I stride manfully onstage and embark on what I feel sure is my side-splittingly amusing, Belgian-themed speechlet. I announce to the crowd that Dries will be producing a new TV show titled *The Real Housewives of Antwerp*. Instead of the usual plastic Barbie dolls, the housewives will be very mopey, artsy, poetic and pale. When disagreements erupt, they will settle arguments by pelting each other with Belgian chocolates.

Funny, right? Apparently not.

The silence in the Celeste Bartos Forum is deafening. You could hear the crickets all the way to Staten Island. If the gowned attendees were chuckling, they were doing it behind their clutch purses.

In a desperate attempt to wring a few laughs out of the assembled fashionrati, I decide to extemporize.

Directly in my field of vision sits a stately, glamorous legend. Mr. André Leon Talley. He is wearing a loosely tied neoclassical turban. It looks like the headgear from a Rembrandt or Ingres painting. The turban in question is classic Talley: seemingly effortless yet over-the-top glamorous. Adorning the turban is a jeweled pin.

HE LOOKS UTTERLY GORGEOUS.

It's worth reflecting on the majesty of Mr. Talley. André Leon Talley is one of the pillars of the fashion community. His knowledge of the nuances of style and his ability to communicate his passions to others is unmatched. He is outrageous and generous and eccentric and extraordinary.

I worship that fabulous, glamorous bitch!

Of all the attendees at this particular awards show, he has displayed the most unbridled panache. And isn't that what fashion is all about?

So why not give him a shout-out?

Moving closer to the mike, I spontaneously suggest that André Leon Talley should "hock the fabulous diamond pin on that turban which you rented to come here tonight," and use the resulting moolah to fund Dries's Antwerp *Housewives* show.

To say that it simply did not work would be accurate.

André is not amused by my en passant reference to his headgear. The phrase "visibly affronted" would best describe his reaction. Ditto his date, Naomi Campbell, who lets out a protective hiss.

My bowels lurch and a vomitaceous feeling engulfs me. Of all the people in that room he—André, the Ab-fabulous, the brilliant, the most life enhancing—was the last person on earth I wished to offend. My intention in singling out this remarkable accessory is to express solidarity with the wearer, the majestically adorned Mr. Talley. Here is an oasis of flamboyance in a sea of formality. I hoped, through the lens of humor, to spotlight ALT and pay homage. My goal—please believe me, André dahling!—was to *j'adore* the shit out of you.

As I staggered back to my seat in a state of dry-mouthed panic, I began to trawl the deep recesses of my consciousness. From whence had sprung this horrid notion of rented accessories? How did I conceive of such a Dada idea?

Then I remembered: Dame Edna, aka Australian comedian and writer Barry Humphries.

In the mid-seventies I wandered into a Knightsbridge bookstore and found Dame Edna Everage, Barry Humphries's alter ego, in housewife drag, autographing a stack of her latest lifestyle tome for a small crowd of admirers. A fan of long standing, I immediately grabbed a book and joined the line.

The lady who preceded me was an aging Sloane Ranger with an entitled air. She seemed to have no idea that she was dealing with a seven-foot Australian bloke in drag and proceeded to ask the author a lot of turgid, probing questions about housewifery, the Australian dried-fruit industry, the climate Down Under and such. When the Sloane declined to purchase a book, the Dame responded by thanking her profusely "for renting that little mink collar to come here and see me today."

Funny and memorable, right?

Back to the turban debacle.

As you can well imagine, I felt ghastly. Sarcasm is no fun unless the audience, victims included, is chuckling right along with you. As a result of my failed attempt, I spent the rest of the evening staring into the middle distance like Whistler's mother. I felt like I should toss my green card out of the window and go back to the Are You Being Served? department store where my fashion journey had begun three decades earlier.

Barely had the sun risen the next morning when peonies were dispatched to Mr. Talley, accompanied by an effusive apology note.

His assistant called mine to say that André would prefer orchids. The hauteur of this response felt like the sharp, stinging smack of an Hermès riding crop, or what I imagine that would feel like were I into sadomasochism. I shivered with humiliation. Before you could say "Inès de la Fressange" or "Princess Gloria von Thurn und Taxis," the substitution was made.

Time is a great healer. In the intervening years, André has seen fit to forgive and forget.

Since André forgave me, I had no choice but to forgive myself. And why not? After all, it was not my fault. The truth of the matter is that I have always had a forked tongue. And I am not to blame. I was raised that way.

I am happy to say that I was barraged with sarcasm during my formative years. My teachers specialized in subtle-but-withering verbal assaults. Many incidents spring to mind. After jackhammering my way through an entire page of *Ulysses* in a robotic monotone—how was I supposed to know that James Joyce expected the reader to insert the lilts, pauses and commas intuitively?—my English teacher announced that he was overcome by the "sensitivity" of my reading and would need to "nip out for a fag" in order to compose himself. While the entire class roared with laughter, I flinched and cringed. But I eventually recovered. Better to be verbally humiliated than whacked upside the head, an outcome which was also on offer.

My home life was equally sarco enriched and sincerity free. I was raised by two members of what Tom Brokaw called the "Greatest Generation" and what I call the "Greatest Sarcastic Generation." When I began to embrace the satins and velvets of glam rock, my parents began pointedly tracking the movements of local traveling circuses and keeping me posted on their whereabouts.

Pops and Mamma saved their best sarcasm for each other, often after drinking vats of homemade sloe gin. Like many dudes of his generation, my dad had a tendency to treat his kids, the fruit of his loins, like some random encumbrance which fate had dumped upon him. My mum was quick to nip this line of thinking in the bud with a little liquor-fueled faux gratitude. "It really was so good of you to take me in off the street, especially with these two children in tow. Have I ever thanked you formally?"

If you were raised amid sarcasm, as opposed to sincerity, you have no choice but to seek out kindred spirits. It's a tribal thing. If you attempt to consort with sincere types, it can only end in mayhem and bloodshed, metaphorically, of course. I knew my Jonny was the one for me when I met his lovely old dad. When I announced my intention to take Jonny white-water rafting, Dad-in-law responded by deadpanning, "Where do you both wish to be buried?"

Sustaining a healthy sarcasm-based relationship is no easy matter and requires effort and creativity. I am fortunate to be married to somebody who is always prepared to go the distance. A couple of months back my Jonny presented me with a greeting card. Naturally, I smelled a rat. He had never given me a card before. Why now? And why was he watching me with such sincere anticipation?

My suspicions were confirmed when I opened the envelope. The inscription, emblazoned across a mumsy floral vista à la Thomas Kinkade, began as follows:

I know how trapped you must feel
In that traitor of a body of yours . . .

I don't recall the rest of the verse. I know that it contained sympathetic commiserations regarding the imprisoning effects of the aforementioned body. I had to admire his ingenuity: repurposing a sincere sympathy card into a lacerating insult—without changing a thing—is an impressive feat of sarcasm.

Delivered via e-mail, Jonny's assault would have lost much of its lethal malevolence. Maybe that's why Karl got so much shit for his remark about Adele. If it had been delivered in person, he could have added a little sarcastic je ne sais quoi.

Bonjour, Adele! Your smartest move would have been to respond to Karl with a bitchy bon mot or two. Given that Karl's comment was fairly straightforward and sarcasm free, you could easily have upstaged him with something really wicked. Just to get your juices going, here is an inspirational example of a Karl slag-off, penned by Barry Humphries—yes, coincidentally, Dame Edna again!—in a recent issue of the *Spectator*:

"It is hard not to pick up a periodical without seeing a picture of Karl Lagerfeld, surely one of the most absurd-looking people on the planet, rivaled only by Colonel Gaddafi and Donald Trump. Herr Lagerfeld is probably a very good dress designer, especially compared with Colonel Gaddafi . . ."

I have no idea if Herr Lagerfeld ever clocked this little gem of a comment. Were he to have read it, I suspect he would have had a good laugh behind his fan, metaphorically of course, since he no longer carries one.

In order to hit the spot and rise above the level of mere insult, sarcasm needs this kind of Wildean panache. Here, for your delectation and inspiration, is one final example of haute couture dissing: Once upon a time, the great Harold Pinter left his *très chic* actress wife, Vivien Merchant, for the aristocratic authoress and grande dame of British letters, Lady Antonia Fraser. His action caused a scandal of epic proportions. One fine day the press knocked on Viv's door and asked her for a comment about

PLATO RIPPED MY BLOUSE

Harold's hasty departure sans wardrobe. La Merchant's sarcastic response gave us Brits a good chuckle.

"Harold didn't need to take a change of shoes," declared the petite thespian, adding, "He can always wear Antonia's. She has very big feet, you know."

Cue the sound of rending flesh.

willi smith
was a
right-on sista

MY ENTIRE BODY was convulsed with racking sobs. There I was, in a public place, a middle-aged dude, openly bawling my eyes out in front of a complete stranger. I was beyond the valley of the *fashion verklempt*.

Not long ago and out of the blue, a CNN journalist invited me out to lunch. She wanted to pick my brain and see if I could help her figure out some pithy way of covering Fashion Week. Her goal was to add a little gravitas to their style-oriented programming. In no time at all, we realized that this was an absurd notion and abandoned it.

During the course of our subsequent meandering conversation, it emerged that we had both lived in Los Angeles for extended periods. She had gone to college there in the early 2000s and I had lived there during the late seventies and early eighties when, as I explained to the young lady, life was freaky, funky and fun. The live-music scene was insane: for ten bucks you could hit the Whisky or the Roxy any night of the week and enjoy the delights of Joy Division, Siouxsie and the Banshees, Nina Hagen or the Cramps or the Psychedelic Furs. You could snag a beat-up car with fins for $500 and an apartment off Hollywood Boulevard for $100 a month.

"Wow. That must have been fabulous."

"Yes, it was totally *amazing* . . . and then it wasn't."

"What happened?"

"All my friends died."

Suddenly, I became overwhelmed with sadness.

That tends to be the way it works. I go for years thinking I have come to terms with that dark and horrible period, and then all of a sudden I access the trauma of the AIDS holocaust, and the tears start to fall.

IN 1982 I TOOK my boyfriend to the doctor.

"It's just an ingrown hair," I said, pointing to the purple mark on his neck.

The doctor had a different diagnosis.

"You have AIDS," he said.

"Can you give my friend a referral to a specialist?" I asked.

"There are no specialists. There is no referral. Are you guys religious?"

Within two years, my pal was dead, and so were many of my other friends, ex-boyfriends and colleagues. To date, more than 600,000 people have died of AIDS in the United States alone.

Thirty years ago, when AIDS arrived, it hit the fashion industry—my people—like a sledgehammer. Readers *d'un cer-*

tain âge will recall how bleak and ghastly it was. Like me, you can only remember those dark days with a mixture of horror and sadness.

To those of you who were not around, I can only say this: You have no idea how lucky you are.

One after another, the brightest and boldest succumbed to this horrifying disease. Our creative pals—some famous, some infamous, most unknown and just starting to hit their stride—perished after being unwittingly infected by the disease of the century. Many died agonizing deaths in the hallways of hospitals without hope or familial support. Back then, in the early days, AIDS really was just like a medieval plague. "Who is next?" was the question on all our lips.

Patrick Kelly, Angel Estrada, Isaia, Adrian Cartmell, Clovis Ruffin, Halston and so many more. AIDS decimated a broad spectrum of the fashion universe. Antonio Lopez and Juan Ramos, Tina Chow, Robert Rose, Peter Lester, Tim Hawkins, Sergio Galeotti, Robert Hayes and Laughlin Barker.

Photographers too: David Seidner, Barry McKinley, Tony Viramontes, Herb Ritts, Bill King, Steven Arnold, Stevie Hughes, Kenneth McGowan and Doug Coder.

And so many of my window-dresser pals: Bob Currie, Michael Cipriano, Cliff Murphy, Colin Burch, Bob Benzio, Stephen Di Petrie, Talmadge the one-namer, and so many more.

These names are just the tip of the iceberg. I cannot list everyone. This book would turn into *War and Peace*.

At the height of this dark and horrible period, I recall visiting a sick friend named Jeffrey Herman. He was a model turned photographer who had just begun to receive some recognition for his pictures. When he fell ill, his life, his hopes, his creativity and his dreams all screeched to a halt.

During Jeffrey's agonizing last days, he expressed a very pessimistic conviction.

"This is the end. We were all headed toward oblivion. Nobody will remember us. We will evaporate. We are dust. We are the lost generation."

I often think about what Jeffrey said and sometimes I wonder if he might not have been correct. Fashion is ephemeral by nature. Today's peacock is tomorrow's feather duster. Fashion is about what's next. What's next? What's next? What's next?

And now that the fashion industry has become this massive, ever-expanding juggernaut, now that we have the twenty-four-hour madness and fabulousness of Internet bloggings and tweetings, now that we have all this distracting meshugaas, it is conceivable that we might forget all the great and talented people who kicked the bucket.

When AIDS struck, the fashion world rallied as never before: Kenneth Cole, Anna Wintour, Donna Karan and Ralph Lauren all did their bit, as did Barneys. I am proud to say we hosted the first retail AIDS fund-raiser at our Seventeenth Street store in the mid-eighties. The philanthropic effort was unprecedented. And the effort continues.

But fund-raising is one thing, and remembrance is another.

When I saw how beautifully the victims of 9/11 were memorialized, I could not help but think also of my fallen heroes. I thought of the bright lights of fashion who were cruelly snuffed out in the 1980s.

And I thought about how important it is for us to keep the flame burning for our friends who slipped away from us over a quarter of a century ago, not just for ourselves, but also for the upcoming generation, many of whom were not even born in 1981.

Upcoming generations need to know that Perry Ellis was a real person, not just a brand name, a beautiful, generous man with long hair and a uniquely poetic vision.

They should know that Moschino is not just a made-up name on a label in the neck of a random frock. Franco Moschino was a true innovator, an Italian surrealist with a wicked wit.

We need to share our memories of talented and inspirational eccentrics like Klaus Nomi, Tommy Rubnitz, Leigh Bowery, Way Bandy and Ricky Wilson of the B-52s. And we need to share the magic and the bravado and the positivity of great fashion designers like Willi Smith.

So let's prove Jeffrey wrong.

Let's know our fashion history and always speak their names and pass on their passion and their legacy.

ENOUGH SOMBER THOUGHTS. Fashion is supposed to be a place of transformation, creativity and joy. Let's end on a positive note.

When it came time to scatter Jeffrey's ashes, I took a portion of them to a windy hilltop near Santa Fe. Like so many fashion people, Jeffrey had a woo-woo side and this was one of his favorite meditation spots. When I reached the summit, I tore open the large FedEx envelope and up-ended it. The ashes all blew back in my direction, frosting my carefully chosen ensemble. This would have amused Jeffrey to no end.

Meanwhile in Rome . . .

Actress Kelly Lynch, a pal of Jeffrey's since her modeling days, took her designated envelope of ashes to the Eternal City. Did she dump them in the Trevi Fountain? Did she sprinkle them from the top of the Colosseum? Did she snort them à la Keith Richards? Hell no.

At the dénouement of the Valentino fashion show, Kelly leapt from her front-row seat and tossed her ash stash onto the runway. Adjacent fashionistas were perplexed. Kelly continued scattering regardless. She knew that this is exactly what Jeffrey would have wanted.

Or was it?

Remembering Jeffrey, with his wicked sense of humor, I think he might well have relished the spectacle of Kelly, the antiheroine of *Drugstore Cowboy*, disposing of his ashes à la Richards.

alexander will need a room

WITH TREMENDOUS RELUCTANCE, I dragged myself out of bed, inserted my eighteenth-century wooden dentures, powdered and deloused my Louis wig, hoisted my lorgnettes in the general direction of my puffy and rheumy eyes and clicked on the TV to watch Kate and Wills tie the knot.

Why the resentful grumpiness and general lack of rejoicing?

Okay, I admit it, I was irate, but with good reason.

Despite being eminently qualified—overqualified, some might say—I had failed to score a lucrative network TV wedding-commentator gig. I saw myself as a shoo-in for a week-long babble fest of piercing insights and romantic royal speculations. If not me, then who? After all, I am both a Brit *and* a queen. Hello!

Yes, I know it sounds tragic, but I actually wanted to be a Royal Watcher. Just for a week. Is that too much to ask?

I have always had a sneaking admiration for those Royal

Watchers—Andrew Morton, Jessica Jayne et al—and their ability to generate endless, speculative, hagiographical poop about the Brit monarchy.

And they make so much money! All the Royal Watchers seem to live in foncy houses, leading me to believe that there is untold wealth to be made in this profession. All you have to do is be smug and effusive and not worry about the fact that, while the Royals are waving to the unwashed masses, you, the Royal Watcher, are waving good-bye to any professional or writerly cred.

When the marriage of Wills and Kate was announced, I braced myself for a deluge of offers. I sat by the phone for days, wearing more tan-fastic maquillage than Bill O'Reilly.

But the phone never rang.

It all seemed so unfair. I was born the year of the coronation. I have watched every royal wedding since the fifties. I sat on the living-room couch staring at the TV while my crazy grandmother stood at attention and waved her hankie at the screen. Don't mock. It's called respect.

And I have a unique perspective on the Royals. I had been accumulating "little-known facts" for years. Did you know, for example, that when Sparky the corgi died, the queen grabbed a shovel and buried him herself on a dark, rain-lashed night? Did you also know that the Queen Mum used to empty her colostomy bag off the balcony at Clarence House and that, as a result, the roses grew abundantly and enthusiastically in this particular location?

I could have peppered my TV coverage with all these texture-adding anecdotes. But no . . .

As the wedding procession began, my mood began to lighten. My wrath dissipated and I got lost in the exquisite pageantry of it all. As I watched Kate Middleton in her Sarah-Burton-for-the-house-of-Alexander-McQueen frock, I found myself moving from rage to melancholia, and not because of the frock, Au contraire! I thought Sarah did a fabulous job. The Elizabethan silhouette—flat and narrow and then exploding majestically from the waist—perfectly suited Kate's tall, skinny body. (This particular style is not for everyone. It would, for example, have turned a shorter bride into a hideous Velázquez dwarf infanta, but on Kate it was pure poetry.)

Yes, the frock was a ten. It was hard to imagine Mr. McQueen doing a better job. As the ceremony progressed, I found myself thinking more and more about the talented and brilliant bloke whose name was on the label. As the music soared, a montage of McQueen memories began to cascade.

Attending an Alexander McQueen fashion show was like taking a stroll through a fashion Fallujah. There was always this magnificent sense of impending catastrophe. Would the gals get electrocuted as they sloshed through all that water? How will the models, in their *Blade Runner*–inspired, condom-tight dresses, navigate those treacherous glass stairs? Answer: They won't. Oops! There goes another one.

I remember one show in particular. The location was a functioning Parisian abattoir. Upon arrival at this house of death, the nostrils of the international fashionrati were assaulted by the unmistakable odor of decaying flesh and animal feces. I noticed some futile last-minute attempts to contend with this problem: PR gals ran back and forth squirting fragrance atomizers.

However, no amount of perfume or Diptyque candles could have made a dent in that all-pervading stench.

The scary-but-fabulous Béatrice Dalle—remember her from the eighties culty movie *Betty Blue?*—sat uncomplainingly in the front row wearing a McQueen bondage dress and an insane thatched wig. It looked as if an English country cottage had landed on her head—in a good way.

The show began. Wearing skintight bondage and leopard-print dresses and sporting wigs like Mademoiselle Dalle's (clearly she was the season's muse and nipped backstage before the show for a little avant-garde coiffure), the gals careened and staggered across the shit-glazed cobblestones.

Many fell. Some clung to the ancient columns of the abattoir for support. Many heels snapped off. Shoes were discarded. It was the perfect McQueen moment: blood, poo, mayhem, carnage and glamour.

Misogynist?

Models can totally handle the McQueen treatment. They are sixteen and fearless and full of champagne. They are having a blast. Besides, Mr. McQueen's short life was more about torturing himself than inflicting pain on highly paid runway chippies.

Alexander McQueen's oeuvre was always informed by the discipline and structure of his early Savile Row tailoring apprenticeship. In the mid-nineties he famously tailored a fantastic coat for David Bowie's *Earthling* tour. The particular design said so much about Alexander. It was a historical garment—sort of like an old footman's coat—cut from a sacred symbol, the flag of the British Empire. Upon completion, Mr. McQueen assaulted it, flung lighter fluid at it and set fire to large chunks of it.

After his tour had finished, Mr. Bowie kindly loaned me this distressed coat-of-many-slashes for a Brit-themed Barneys window. The year was 1997—the zenith of that whole Cool Britannia moment—and this particular display was packed with eccentric tchotchkes evoking the land of my birth.

The back wall of the window consisted of a portrait gallery titled "The Great Queens of England." Victoria and Elizabeths I and II all rubbed shoulders with Boy George, Quentin Crisp, Oscar Wilde, John Galliano and Alexander McQueen.

I felt strongly that Alexander deserved to be part of this group, especially since his Bowie coat was dominating the display. Even though Alexander was the new kid on the block, he had already established himself as an influential provocateur in the tradition of Vivienne Westwood. He had invented, among other things, the "bumster" pant, which ultimately spawned the ubiquitous buttcrack jean. I had never met him but assumed he was as bold and ballsy as his creativity would suggest.

Alexander happened to make a trip to New York at the time the window was installed. He was not yet thirty. I ran into him at an event, which he attended with his beloved mum, Joyce, on his arm. (Her death, three days before his, is viewed by many as the main trigger for his suicide. Other writers suggested that he always wrestled with suicidal thoughts, but that he had waited till Mum went first.)

I introduced myself and asked him if he had seen the window. Knowing that he was an East End working-class lad, the son of a taxi driver, I expected a little cheeky badinage, a cocky Cockney riposte. Alexander surprised me by quietly voicing genuine concern that, as happy as he was to see his coat on display, he had recently lost some weight and the portrait I had used made him look fatter than he was. He looked genuinely hurt.

Instead of a bold, gay, punk-rock provocateur, I saw the vulnerable kid, the self-described "pink sheep" of his family, the lad who had been bullied at school and called McQueer.

A few years after the tubby portrait, a slimmed-down Alexander was scheduled to travel once more to New York to relaunch his menswear collection. McQueen menswear had, up to this point, always been a bit of problem. Initial attempts were bold, flamboyant and a tad too costumey for American dudes. Other than Bowie, it's hard to imagine who would need a floor-length glen-plaid Edwardian coat with a chrysanthemum embroidered on the back. It was also hard to imagine Alexander himself wearing it. He always seemed to dress like a London wide boy, with his shaved head, trainers, Fred Perry, etc.

At Barneys we were excited about the newly revamped men's collection and anxious to have Alexander host a launch event at the store. In preparation for the party, we had a meeting with a McQueen PR operative. This is when the famous phrase was spoken which was to reverberate through the halls of Barneys corporate office for many years.

"Alexander will need a room . . . a room where he can do his drugs."

Sounding a bit like Lady Bracknell—"Drugs?" "A room?"—we expressed our discomfort with this request and pointed out the illegality thereof. Sorry, but we simply could not oblige. PS: Are you people out of your minds?

The party date arrived and Alexander was a no-show. This

ended up being less of a catastrophe than one would imagine. If any guest asked me where he was, I just kept saying, "Oh! He's here somewhere. Maybe he nipped to the loo . . ."

While Alexander was MIA, his clothing was not. The new men's collection, though still edgy, was much more wearable. Alexander got better at everything he did, except looking after his own mental health. Clearly that was beyond his control. There is no doubt that, had he lived, he would have gone on to become a titan of twenty-first-century design.

His suicide leaves us all, his adoring fans, clutching at straws and theorizing and burbling and speculating like a bunch of frenzied Royal Watchers. We want to know why. With international success, a groovy pad in Mayfair and an assured place in the eternal fashion pantheon, why did he kill himself?

People kill themselves for lots of different reasons. My uncle Dave was driven to suicide by fear. He swallowed a handful of my auntie's pills to escape a bunch of gangsters—coincidentally, these were blokes from Alexander's area of London—who were coming to collect their debts. Uncle Dave knew they would chop his nuts off when they found out he was flat broke. So he did the job for them.

My grandfather—not the toothless Irish one, the other one—also killed himself. His circumstances might have been more akin to Alexander's. An astrologer by trade, he was a sensitive bloke who suffered from unrelenting depression. One day he got his hands on a gun and ended it all. He felt he had no alternative.

I'm not sure why Alexander never showed up at Barneys.

Let's cut him a little retroactive slack and assume it was a scheduling conflict as opposed to a disinclination to attend an event where there was no designated room to toot.

I have a theory about Mr. McQueen. Growing up gay in working-class Britain, regardless of how loving your immediate family might be, is no bloody picnic. I was fortunate to escape to a land where it's okay to go to a psychotherapist and attempt to unravel your early traumas. Introspection and psychotherapy are not part of British culture. Alexander used his work to exorcize his demons and for a while it worked. Then it wasn't enough.

The fact that Alexander became so successful did nothing to diminish his torments. It merely increased them. The more successful he got, the bigger the dissonance between who he was— rich, creative, living up West and creating chiffon magic for rich women—and who his butch, gritty East End, Fred Perry–wearing roots said that he should be. No amount of drugs or booze could ease the conflict and the pain.

In addition to all the gay stuff, Alexander's psyche was further tormented by the British class system. He was drawn to the pageantry and the toffs (aristo Isabella Blow, who also committed suicide, was his muse), but he was repelled and enraged by their assumed superiority. While finishing up a bespoke jacket for Prince Charles, he allegedly stitched a label that read I'M A CUNT into the lining.

Et voilà! A young bloke compelled to leave the macho of the East End for the safety and magic of the effete fashion milieu, living it, loving it, ashamed of it and loathing it all at the same time. The creative rage, soaring imagination and intense curiosity that Mr. McQueen exhibited throughout his career were functions of all these painful contradictions.

Drugs. Drugs. Drugs. The fashion world has no shortage of booze and dope. Drugs were part of the picture. But they were not the cause of his suicide. He used them to escape his feelings of guilt, shame and despair. To my amateur Freudian gaze, his suicide by hanging reads like an act of self-administered capital punishment, a punishment for crimes that the complex, sensitive, lovely lad never committed in the first place.

Watching fashion shows today, I always find myself thinking about Alexander McQueen. I miss his explosive creativity. Where are the torment and the drama today? They are simply not there. The comfy self-acceptance currently enjoyed by today's emerging designers does not produce that kind of fabulous madness. Designers today are too happy and too well adjusted to produce great art. I am happy that they are happy, but I cannot help missing the blood and the mayhem and the rage and the broken heels.

zips up the back with no bones

ALL OF A SUDDEN I SPOT HER.

She is alone and she is moving quickly toward us, weaving and gliding through the chairs and tables.

I am sitting in a bijou lunch spot. I am munching on a nice lobster salad. My Jonny is having a wafer-thin chicken paillard. We are in Florida.

The youngish woman is getting closer. She has the malevolent sense of purpose which one associates with suicide bombers. Wait a minute. Maybe she *is* a suicide bomber. Or maybe she is the irate wife who is about to publicly confront her cheating husband and serve him divorce papers or pump him full of bullets. Or maybe she is a professional hit girl. Her steely gaze and her sucked-in cheeks suggest that she might well be a hired assassin. Her intimidating demeanor runs in sharp contrast to her designer ensemble. Clearly she has disguised herself as an upscale socialite to avoid detection.

As she approaches, looking haunted yet blank, I prepare for the worst. Something horrid is about to happen. A bomb? An acid attack? An age-old grievance finally coming home to roost as machine-gun fire destroys the peaceful mise-en-scène?

Everything goes into slow motion.

I brace myself and prepare to dive under the table.

Already I am overwhelmed by the feeling that this is a watershed historical moment. If I survive, then I know that this will be the beginning of an entirely new chapter in history. Everything will be pegged on this date: events will be described as occurring before or after this terrible incident. Like the Kennedy assassination, this will be a where-were-you-when moment.

"The suit is by Calvin Klein. The shoes and bags are from the new resort collections at Neiman Marcus."

Sheeesh! That's a relief. She's not a jihadist at all.

She's modeling, informally. She is, in fact, an *informal model*.

What we are witnessing is not the prelude to homicidal mayhem, but rather an unexpected burst of informal modeling. That is, modeling that is not formal; that is, modeling that is not on a runway; that is, modeling that is occurring for the benefit of nobody in particular. This kind of modeling is for the universe. That's how informal it is.

Informal modeling is an age-old practice. Models have been informally gliding between tables of fine-diners for decades. I am not sure exactly when it first started. It seems like something the Romans would have dug. I can just see Calpurnia, Messalina, Livia and the rest of the girls lolling about eating their honey-dipped dormice while some vestal beauties flaunted the latest toga styles.

I first took note of informal modeling in the 1939 Joan Craw-ford movie *The Women*. In one particular scene an informal model flits among the gossiping denizens of the upscale beauty parlor, chirping robotically to nobody in particular.

"Our new one-piece foundation garment zips up the back with no bones . . . our new one-piece foundation garment zips up the back with no bones . . . our new one-piece foun . . . ," ad nauseam.

Informal modeling is like street theater, minus the BO. (Who among us has not had an imprisoning experience with an inter-active mime in a stale costume?) Though informal models have much in common with mimes and performance artists, there is one group which they have even more in common with: escaped mental patients.

Informal models and mental patients are indistinguishable in many regards. Both groups move, walk and talk while inhabit-ing imaginary situations: I am in a parade; I am on a cruise ship; I am staring at the horizon; I am stopping and twirling on the street for no reason; I am not walking normally. Why would I?

Informal models and mentally ill people both smile enig-matically at people they do not know—and at nothing. Both groups approach complete strangers with exaggerated familiar-ity. They allow people to touch their clothing. They smile re-lentlessly.

Not all mentally ill people behave like informal models. My grandmother, she of the lobotomy, used to get into an occasional snit and throw household appliances. Other than that she never did anything remotely modelish. My schizophrenic uncle Ken, on the other hand, was more than a little mannequinesque: he often struck poses and attitudes. He was also very handsome and skinny and wore rumpled clothing. Could he have been an informal male model? Unfortunately, his hunky youth preceded the Abercrombie years, otherwise Ken would have been a shoo-in for the role of a welcoming, groin-baring A&F host. Like many schizophrenics, he was temperature oblivious and would have thought nothing of standing shirtless at a store entrance.

Call me a killjoy, but I have never been a proponent of informal modeling. Formal modeling? Bring it on! But informal modeling is undeniably poignant and kind of sad. When I encounter an informal model, my heart is filled with *tristesse*. Could there be anything more heartrending than the idea of a gal—maybe a former local beauty queen or ex–weather reader on local TV—walking around a local lunch spot looking well turned out but dazed, and clutching a card that reads:

CONTEMPORARY SEPARATES

or

MARINA RINALDI—larger sizes available

or

MOTHER OF THE BRIDE—now on sale

?

Informal modeling is tinged with desperation. An informal model is a gal who masquerades for a living. By day, she's a dressed-up glamourpuss, living the highlife and reeking of prosperity. At night, she returns to a life of film-noir misery. She goes home to her lonely walk-up, where she futzes with her manicure and covers her face in cold cream. Once a week her married boyfriend comes over for a glass of amaretto and a quick jiggle. It's all too tragic.

For these reasons, I have always shied away from informal modeling. Until . . .

When the Barneys women's store opened on Seventeenth Street in 1986, it was big news. This part of Manhattan was still largely ungentrified. Hookers and drug dealers were never far away. The idea of selling Chanel suits and Valentino frocks below Twenty-third Street was audacious.

In order to lure well-heeled customers downtown, we knew we had to make the place unique. We all agreed that the store should be a welcoming, warm space with a chic residential vibe. The Pressman family instructed us specifically on this issue: they were vociferous about the fact that they wanted customers to feel as if they were *shopping in somebody's home.*

Converting a block of co-ops into retail square footage was not without its problems, not the least of which was the fact that many residents were reluctant to vacate. Rehousing these tenants was a lengthy and complex process. Some were happy to move on to pastures new. Others, despite the generous rehousing terms, resented the involuntary change.

Opening day arrived. TV cameras positioned themselves to capture this historic moment of gentrification. Suddenly, a contingent of pissed-off former tenants materialized. They had come to demonstrate against what they saw as the intrusion of unwanted luxury commerce in their lives. They began to chant. As customers entered, their ears were assailed with improbably apropos shouts.

"You're shopping in somebody's home!"

"You're shopping in somebody's home!"

"You're shopping in somebody's home!"

The irony of the heckling was not lost on those of us who had worked so hard to give the store that superchic residential vibe.

Despite the demos, the store was a howling success. The lower-level restaurant—in retail we never use the word "basement" unless it is in conjunction with the word "bargain"—was named Le Café. Absurd, I know, especially given the un-Frenchy nature of the neighborhood, but it seemed like a good idea at the time.

Despite the name, Le Café was packed. It became the destination du jour. It was almost *too* successful. Many patrons were lolling about in the restaurant for hours and leaving the store without checking out the floors of designer goodies above. Why not try to give them a taste of the clothing while they were eating?

The store owner decreed that, if madam was reluctant to leave the restaurant, then the designer goodies would/should/could come to madam. "Informal modeling! That's the answer."

With much trepidation, I called my pal Mona. She was a pale blonde who looked like a latter-day Veronica Lake. Mona had never done any informal modeling before. She was a formal model. Very formal, in fact. The fave of photogs like David Seidner, Mona was known for her snooty, haughty attitudes and exaggerated Dovima poses.

Despite her lack of informal modeling experience, I felt that Mona was the right gal for the job. Nobody would ever mistake Mona for a mime or a suicide bomber. And she could mimic the idea of an old-fashioned informal model. She could informally model, *as if* she were informally modeling. She could, in other words, deliver a cool parody. Her knowing attitude would, hopefully, make the entire undertaking less tragic and frightening, and protect her from potential mockery by hipper-than-thou downtowners.

I told Mona she should arrive at the store around eleven o'clock on Saturday morning. One of the display guys would be waiting for her with an incentivizing check and a rolling rack of designer must-haves. He would help her to dress. She would don a succession of outfits, swoop down the stairs into the restaurant and then whoosh back up again.

With every outfit change, she would be given a new card to hold, bearing the name of the designer on display. These cards were to be printed ahead of time in the display studio on our ancient sign-making machine.

I loathed this machine. A more annoying piece of equipment would have been hard to find. No matter how carefully you prepped the sign—setting the metal blocks, meticulously rolling the type with oil-based ink and then inserting the pristine white pieces of card—the signs always turned out smudgy and wonky. In order to get one perfect sign, you were obliged to print about fourteen.

I planned on hiding out on the day of Mona's debut. There were no cell phones back then. I would wait till she got home in the evening and give her a call just to make sure she had not committed suicide. Why wasn't I there to support her? Better that she face the agony of informal modeling on her own rather than have me cringing and waving on the sidelines like a crazed pageant mother.

Curiosity eventually got the better of me. At about three o'clock I roused myself from the fetal position and headed to the store.

Mona was nowhere to be seen.

Suddenly, I heard a kerfuffle on the second floor and looked up.

Mona appeared and began to descend the staircase. She looked like a blonde Audrey Hepburn in *Funny Face*. From a distance she appeared poised and regal, like a haughty Betty Draper bitch. As she approached, I noticed that customers began stepping quickly aside to let her pass. They were staring at her in an alarmed fashion.

As she got closer, things went from *Funny Face* to *Sunset Boulevard*. Mona was Gloria Swanson, having totally lost her marbles, vamping down the stairs toward her cruel fate.

"I'm ready for my close-up, Mr. DeMille."

Just like Norma Desmond's audience, Mona's audience was looking at her as if she were nuts.

As she got closer, I began to understand why.

One hand was on her hip and the other was holding a depressingly smudgy sign bearing one smudgy word.

NOWHERE.

Informal modeling is Dada and strange at the best of times. Mona's enigmatic message took it to another level.

"It's the designer label—NOWHERE! That's the name of the clothing collection," pleaded Mona, to no avail.

I did not believe her.

I knew that Mona and her sign were making a much more profound statement about life, and that this was—paging Jean-

Paul Sartre!—a moment of the purest existential nausea. And I felt a wave of solidarity with Mona. After all, aren't we all, in some way or other, just informal models, winding and smiling our way through time and space, absurdly twirling and posing, and headed . . . nowhere?

acknowledgments

HEARTFELT THANKS to the following people, without whom this book may or may not have been possible.

My Blue Rider/Penguin publishing family: David, Sarah, Aileen and Brian.

My Barneys fashion family: Mark, Daniela, Charlotte, Tom, Dennis, Chris, Beth, Tommy, Matt, Rick, Sabrina, Benj, Lauren, Sav, Mary Olive, Jessica, Tomm, Courtney, Becky, Rena, Will, Emily, Elise, Tracey, Dina, Jay, Wanda, Tomoko, Laura, Marc, Vinnie, and anyone whose name I forgot, plus all the salespeople and managers in all the stores, plus Richard and Lisa, who are very groovy and just happen to own the joint.

My Slate.com family: Jacob (+ Needles) and David and Chad and Julia.

My actual family: Jonny, Mommie, Wretch, Dave, Nessy,

Lenn, Harry the piglet, Leila, Aaron, Sheel, Gypsy, Tanya, Joyce F., and Deb.

Last but not least, I would like to acknowledge Liberace, the geriatric Norwich terrier who has kept me company while I wrote this book and who will hopefully make it to pub date. Fingers crossed.

about the author

SIMON DOONAN is the creative ambassador for Barneys New York and the author of several books, including *Gay Men Don't Get Fat*, *Wacky Chicks*, and *Beautiful People* (published in the U.S. as *Nasty*), which became a BBC TV series. Originally from England, he worked on Savile Row, at Maxfield in Los Angeles, and with Diana Vreeland at the Costume Institute of the Metropolitan Museum of Art before becoming the creative director of Barneys New York, where he designed legendary window displays for more than twenty years. In 2009, he designed the holiday decorations for the Obama's first White House Christmas. Formerly a columnist for *The New York Observer*, he is now a contributor to Slate.com, and has appeared on *Gossip Girl*, *Iron Chef America*, *America's Next Top Model*, and elsewhere. Doonan lives in New York with his husband, Jonathan Adler.